INDIRA GANDHI
The Last Post

INDIRA GANDHI
The Last Post

KHWAJA AHMAD ABBAS

BOMBAY
POPULAR PRAKASHAN

POPULAR PRAKASHAN PRIVATE LIMITED
35-C, Pandit Madan Mohan Malaviya Marg,
Popular Press Bldg., Tardeo, Bombay 400 034

First Published 1985
Reprinted 1989

(3323)

ISBN 0 86132 116 2

Printed in India by
Ram Printograph (India)
C-114, Industrial Area Okhala
Phase I, New Delhi 110 020

Published by
RAMDAS G. BHATKAL
Popular Prakashan Pvt. Ltd.
35-C, Pandit Madan Mohan Malaviya Marg
Popular Press Bldg., Tardeo, Bombay 400 034

❀

Preface

I WANT to make it clear that this book, *The Last Post*, is the third and the final one in the series starting with *The Return of The Red Rose* (published in 1966) and *That Woman*, first published in 1973, being the second one. The present publisher will bring together, all the three books in one volume entitled *Life and Death of Indira Gandhi* which will be the definitive and complete biography of Indira Gandhi.

I tried to write the biography, as objectively as possible with considerable sympathy, but never succumbed to fulsome flattery, which some other authors did! Nor did I, even while she was out-of-power, mock at her or condemn her outright.

In my opinion, she was a very human being, being a mixture of a lot of good—courage to stand by her convictions, even if they were bad ones, and some weak points—which were not major ones.

I have compared her with President Roosevelt who was also a mixture of good and bad.

I have tried to catalogue all her characteristics in the last chapter of the book—*Verdict*—which were attributed to her by her flatterers and carping critics.

The Epilogue is based on an exclusive interview I had with Prime Minister Rajiv Gandhi on May 29, 1985.

I am grateful to Mr. R.K. Karanjia, the Chief Editor of *BLITZ*, for allowing me to use material which I had written on my own LAST PAGE.

I must also acknowledge the cooperation that I received from my publisher, Mr. Ramdas Bhatkal, who continues the liberal traditions of his father, the late Mr. G.R. Bhatkal.

K.A. ABBAS

28 June 1985

Contents

1

☸

Indira Gandhi: The Last Post

CALL IT chance or destiny, but I was in Delhi on 31st October 1984. The Soviet Land Nehru Award Committee's final meeting had been called up on the previous day. I had arrived one day earlier to spend some time with my nephew and nieces.

On Sunday morning, I borrowed a car to go to Rohtak in Haryana to meet a friend whom I had never met before but with whom I had prolonged correspondence. She was the City Magistrate of Rohtak. While taking us out to lunch, Jayawanti's correct behaviour made a great impression on me. She was neither too officious nor too polite, and yet she had womanly grace. I found out that with her husband, a Professor of English in the local college, she does inspire confidence among her people—the Haryanvis.

"Are you the only female City Magistrate?", I asked her.

"Certainly not", she answered me.

"In India, there must be dozens of them. I think in Haryana and Punjab, we are the second batch of civil servants. After all, we are inspired by the best and the greatest civil servant in this country—I am referring to the example of the Prime Minister, Mrs. Indira Gandhi."

I drove back to Delhi that afternoon, marvelling at the way we have made progress in agriculture. The conventional cluster of mud huts was nowhere to be seen. We must have passed by at least a dozen villages but there was not a single mud hut along the road. Each village had pucca houses and shops whose peasant proprietors moved about on cycles and scooters, and the most hopeful sign of prosperity was the tractors. The cycle age has been passed, now we are in the scooter and tractor age!

After this hopeful and optimistic glimpse of rural India, I felt elated but tired. Next morning was the meeting of the Central Committee of the Soviet Land Nehru Awards. Barring a member from South India, all the other members were present, along with the new Chairman, T.N. Kaul, whom I knew since his days in Moscow. We had a thorough discussion with all the candidates for the Awards and we selected three First Prize Award winners. One of these was Mrs. Godavari Parulekar, the 77-year old lady who is a Marxist-Communist worker among the Warli Scheduled Tribes in Maharashtra. The 3-hour discussion was resolved by Mr. Kaul and we were all free to do what we individually wished to do.

"When are you leaving?" asked Sushila, the Secretary of the Committee.

"I still do not know", I said.

"I have to meet some people here. Then I will decide." I promised to let her know beforehand—may be the next day.

I had lunch with my old friend, Suresh Kohli, and Charlie who is as old as the hills, now cultural counsellor of *Patriot* and *Link* papers.

"Drop in at our office today or, if you are here, the day after", said Charlie.

I had told him that I would gladly do so but that I did not know when. Suresh told him that I could not leave abruptly since he had arranged my interview with the All India Radio people and that he thought that T.V. people would not be far behind.

"He shall not go tomorrow!", Suresh spoke with authority.

So the indecision about the booking of my ticket to Bombay continued till the morning of the 31st. Suresh was to pick me up in a taxi to go to the Broadcasting House. We had barely finished our breakfast when the honk of his taxi was heard. I promptly hobbled down from my nephew's first floor flat and got into the taxi with Suresh.

I looked at my watch. The time was 9-18 a.m.

"Broadcasting House *chalo*", ordered Suresh and the taxi

leapt forward.

"What time have we got to be there", I asked, knowing that we were already late.

The lady producer was waiting for us in the portico when we arrived at the outer gate of the Broadcasting House which was closed, guarded by a sentry.

"Where are your passes?", demanded the sentry brusquely.

"That lady there is waiting for us with the passes", Suresh pointed at the portico.

"You can go there on foot, but I cannot let this taxi to go in."

Suresh pointed to my left leg and explained that I had pain in my foot and could not walk. The sentry would not yield. So I got down from the taxi and started walking with some difficulty on the gravelled path, holding on to Suresh.

Now, at the inner gate of the Broadcasting House, we were stopped again.

"Passes *laiye*", the sentry again asked. The lady producer put her hand in her bag and pulled out her identity card that allowed her to take any one inside on her own responsibility.

"I have to escort them to the V.I.P. Room", she said. "After that I will prepare their passes."

I looked at my watch. The time was exactly 10 a.m.

Arrived at the V.I.P. Reception Room, the senior lady producer made a beeline for the intercom. She picked up the receiver and asked for her senior. She was told that for the time being all telephone connections—both internal as well as external—were under 'suspension'.

"What is happening?, she asked.

"For the last fifteen minutes, all telephonic conversation is forbidden."

"Come in, Mr. Abbas, with me alone to the Studio", said the lady producer, putting down the receiver. What I could not understand was why one of the sentries walked behind me to the Talks Studio. I was escorted by two lady producers and the senior producer. The two juniors were to ask me some questions while the senior one supervised from the adjacent Recording Room.

The interview started immediately.

[3]

But I was between two of my beings. One-half of me was mechanically answering questions on literature—specially the progressive literature and films and other things, while the other was cross-questioning in my own: 'What is happening? Why this tight security? Why the Sikh taxi driver could not bring me to the portico? Why this hush-hush hustle and bustle? Why is there different treatment today? After all, I was a frequent visitor to the Broadcasting House. Never before have I been treated like this.'

At last the interview was over. The two young things heaved a sigh of relief and they vanished. The senior lady producer was walking beside me in the corridor that would bring us back to the V.I.P. Room.

At last she whispered to me "The Prime Minister has been shot in her stomach."

"How is she?", I asked. The journalist in me was suddenly awakened.

"She is in the All India Medical Institute", she still whispered back to me.

"Surgeons are trying to take out the bullets."

"How many are there?"

"Sixteen."

"Sixteen!"

The whole Broadcasting House was revolving around me. I was stunned and I was unable to ask any more questions.

"Has the news been broadcast?", I asked after a time.

"Yes—There is a mob of would-be blood donors surrounding the Medical Institute, all clamouring to offer their blood."

I felt relieved.

"Her blood is not easy to match", she added. "It is of a rare count, and one of those with the same blood group was her killer who has himself been killed!"

Just then one of her junior colleagues caught up with her, whispered something to her and disappeared.

"The news has come", said the senior producer.

"She has expired on the operation table." I looked again at my watch. The time was exactly 12 noon. The whole drama had taken less than three hours.

But we were not allowed to leave the Broadcasting House. Coffee was ordered—and it took time to arrive. Then the senior producer took time to make it. Then, ceremoniously, the coffee cups were handed to all present. At last coffee cups were drained. Meanwhile, an elaborate tape recorder was wheeled in and set up in front of me.

"Mr. Abbas, you knew the Prime Minister personally. So we will begin with your *Shraddhanjali*."

I began:

"When Mahatma Gandhi was assassinated, Jawaharlal Nehru climbed the gate of Birla House and he said, 'The light has gone out of our lives.'

"When Jawaharlal Nehru died, *Blitz* headlined the Obituary 'NEHRU LIVES'.

"So, in this case, what can I say except to combine those words and say:

"The light has gone out of our lives but Indira Gandhi is not dead, despite sixteen bullets in her body. SHE LIVES—in all her work, her projects she had started, in the people whom she saved from disastrous floods and famines and inter-communal riots."

It was nearly 2 in the afternoon and we were released from detention in the Broadcasting House. Now there was no NEWS to be protected. It was travelling all over the city from one mouth to another's ears. The newspapers were out with special supplements proclaiming the shattering spot news: INDIRA DEAD— VICTIM OF HER OWN SECURITY!

The Connaught Place was deserted—all shops and restaurants were closed. But people were there—talking, gesticulating, clustered in groups, small or big.

Who were the assassins? Somebody blurted out: "Why, the Sardars, of course!" There was an ominous ring of threat underscoring the 'of course'.

So, it was connected with what happened four months ago at the Golden Temple in Amritsar—the Operation Blue Star! That, they think, has been avenged by the death of this frail but graceful little woman! But it required sixteen bullets to be pumped into her, first with a revolver and, as if that was not enough, then with a sten-gun. The other Gandhi required only four bullets

[5]

from the revolver held by a Maharashtrian youth, Nathuram Godse. Raising his hand in benediction, the Mahatma said "He Ram!" and was silenced for ever.

This great little woman in a Yogic saffron-coloured sari she had picked for herself from her wardrobe had just walked out of her house. She had got herself made up—after all, she had to be ready for her Video interview in her office just across the road, practically in the same house. The camera and its crew were waiting—including the famous Actor-Director Peter Ustinov. That is why, presumably, she had not worn her bulletproof jacket.

How did the assassins get the news that the 'Madame' would not be wearing her bulletproof jacket that day? Who could have told them? The make-up woman, or two of her assistants who were the last of the persons to see Mrs. Gandhi before she set off for her Akbar Road Office?

She was three minutes late already. Normally, she was always punctual. The Actor-Producer was with her for two days during her Orissa tour and, each time, she had checked with his watch to ensure that she was punctual to the split-second. Now she had to be before the cameras at 9-15 and it was already past that time. Ustinov looked at his watch. It showed 9-17. She was delayed for the time it took to call her servant and to tel' him to give her guests a hot cup of tea. Water was always kept boiling on the gas-stove because the Madame would order tea or coffee for her guests at any odd time of the day or night. But now it was only the hour after breakfast. So she gave elaborate instructions to the servant, and only after she was assured that her guests would be well looked after, she set out to cross the lawn and came to the wicket-gate.

Beant Singh, Sub-Inspector of Security, was there to open the gate for her. He folded his hands in a gesture of *Namaskar*. His folded hands had hidden a revolver exactly as Godse, the murderer of Mahatma Gandhi, had done. Seconds later, as Sub-Inspector Beant Singh unfolded his hands, she saw a revolver clinched in his right hand. She was not alarmed or even surprised, as he was on security duty and they always had arms with them, concealed from the public.

[6]

Within three seconds, she had a flash-back of what she had written on his file, when someone higher-up in the security had suggested in writing that Beant Singh and the other Sikh—What was his name? Something like Satwant Singh or Satyendra Singh? —be relieved of their duties from the Prime Minister's Security Guard because of their Sikh religion. She had scribbled in her handwriting:

"Am I a secular head of a secular State or not?"

That was all, she thought. And in that moment, she felt a bullet piercing her garments. She could not count the bullets as the blood spluttered out of the fatal holes, she fell down on the lawn. She was not yet unconscious; so from her position, she had an ant's eye-view of the Sepoy Satwant Singh—now, she was positively certain of his name—holding a sten-gun at the ready. Seconds later, that sten-gun was spewing out bullets at a fast pace. She was shocked at the casual manner in which he was firing his sten-gun. And before he had exhausted the magazine, she became unconscious. The last question that came to her mind: But I am glad, I am destined to die like Gandhiji—but why? Why? WHY?

Sonia Gandhi picked up the bullet riddled body and carried it to the White Ambassador and strangely enough it was another Sikh, the driver of her car who raced it to the AIIMS. The doctor-in-charge summoned all the cardiac surgeons in the Institute.

"VVIP ON TABLE IN THE OPERATION THEATRE. GREAT EMERGENCY. ALL CARDIAC SURGEONS AND NURSES TO COLLECT THERE AT ONCE. COME IN YOUR PYJAMAS IF YOU ARE NOT DRESSED. IT IS SUCH AN EMERGENCY."

This was the latest and the biggest EMERGENCY call-up. The lift to the Seventh Floor was soon full of doctors and nurses. Those who reached the lift a little later had to climb the stairs, taking two steps in one.

When they reached the Operation Theatre they scrubbed and put on their surgical robes and masks which were kept ready for them.

Now they were around the table on which the patient's body riddled by bullets was laid out. One of them thought of something, but waited for his superior's orders. He said, "Mouth-to-

[7]

mouth Resuscitation, Sir?"

"Go ahead and do it."

The doctor took a long breath, applied his lips to the Prime Minister's lips and exhaled the air from his lungs.

The crowd outside knew nothing of what was going on inside. They were mostly silent, or murmuring their prayers to their different Gods and His Messengers—Shiva, Rama, Zoroaster, Christ, Allah and Mohammed were invoked; but in vain! Soon the crowd sensed that she who was taken in had died on the operation table. The prayers were instantly muffled by sobs. How did they guess it? From the faces of the VIPs who were slowly coming out? But still they stood there helplessly.

The would-be blood-donors were disappointed. They could have at least given their blood! That would have given them some consolation. At least they owed that much to her. Still they waited in silence. The body had to be carried out, some time. They stayed there, waiting for their chance to have a glimpse of her.

The elder, and now the only, son of the Prime Minister came by 4.00 p.m. He was on a tour of West Bengal. And then came Sardar Zail Singh, the President of India, who had just cut short his trip to the Middle East.

The newspapers came out with their Black Border supplements carrying the news of her death. Now, no longer was it a rumour. The newspapers cannot tell such a BIG, BIG Lie!

Five hours later, we were returning to our Defence Colony flat, having a perfunctory look at the dead city and its lifeless heartland, Connaught Circus. There is a Police barrier near Defence Colony, where the cars have to take a turn to the left on entering the Colony. This evening, there was no Police.

Policemen, we had not yet seen. But there were nearly a dozen young men who seemed well-clothed and prosperous-looking.

[8]

They had stopped five cars already and our car was the sixth. The amateurs had long-handled electric torches in their hands. It was apparent that they were looking for "Sardars". They were flashing the circle of light from their torches. Behind us, on the back seat of the car, were two-and-a-half women—if child Zeba is to be counted as half a female. They were my two nieces and the daughter of one of them. On the front seat, we were two-and-a-half males, if my grand nephew Mansoor is to be counted as half a male.

It was obvious that none of us could be mistaken for a Sikh. The idea was to get Rs. 25 from each Hindu or Muslim who was held up by these amateur Police. Still each of the hoodlums cast the circle of light at all the six faces in the car. May be, they wanted to ensure that we were not *Sardars*-in-hiding. When my face was briefly illuminated, there was a small argument amongst them in which I could identify one crucial word: *Blitz*. May be, I was identified, and they were literate enough not to hold the writer of the *LAST PAGER* in *Blitz* to ransom. So, they let us go. Whether they got Rs. 25 from the other cars which were held up or not, would not be known. May be, the occupants of those cars willingly or unwillingly gave them money, for the young men were quite outspoken. "We want to buy oil, we have to burn some Sardars."

They were the first of thousands of such people on the roads let loose that night. What they did with the oil they bought from the money they collected was apparent, when we saw empty shells of six burnt out trucks standing in a row. They were the property of a *Sardar*. Heaps of torn and burnt clothes were scattered in front of the house of the proprietor of those trucks.

Were they mad in their grief? Or were they emotionless hoodlums who wanted to kill and burn the *Sardars* for a change?

At twelve that night, Rajiv Gandhi spoke in a composed and restraining language in his first broadcast as the new Prime Minister. He spoke of his mother, who was, in a sense, the mother of the whole country. He was consoling each one of us. He certainly never gave no good wishes to those hoodlums to burn the Sardars or their property!

Thousands of such hoodlums were killing Sikhs that night,

killing them and, what was worse, humiliating them by shaving off their religious symbols—their beards and long hair. Cigarette lighters were often used to set fire to their beards and the hair on their heads.

Were they avenging the massacre of Hindus in Punjab?

Indira Gandhi did not allow the Hindus of Haryana to take the law in their own hands! An Indian is an Indian, whether he be a Hindu, or a Muslim, or a Christian, or a Sikh, or a Parsi!

The first commandment is still remembered: "THOU SHALT NOT KILL"!

2

⚜

Prelude to Emergency

"I do not love the money. What is one getting out of it? What other interest can you suggest to me? I do not read. What can I do?"

PHILIP D. ARMOUR

RAJIV GANDHI, the elder son of the Prime Minister, Indira Gandhi, joined the Indian Airlines as a Junior Pilot and flew Night Air Mail. Dakotas. Right upto 1982 he worked as a Pilot while still living with his mother, the Prime Minister. Quite a democratic set-up !

But Sanjay Gandhi, the younger son, had other ambitions. He would be the Henry Ford of India. He would manufacture a car of his own. So, in Gulabi Bagh, Sanjay rented a garage from a car mechanic and converted this into a workshop. With a few hired mechanics he worked ten to twelve hours a day, even in summer, hammering out a car with the help of a second-hand engine and with odds and ends of car-parts purchased from *kabadi* shops of the Jumma Masjid area.

When the car was at last 'assembled' or 'manufactured', the proud son gave a lift in it to his mother. He might not be a scholar or a thinker; but now, at last he had demonstrated that he was certainly a 'doer'. He boasted to a newspaper editor that he read only comics and never anything serious such as his grandfather Jawaharlal Nehru's books. Indeed, he seemed to have developed

[11]

an allergy, even contempt, for Nehru's ideas and ideals embodied in his books. He had no need for them.

The car was named Maruti after the monkey God. The story of Maruti is too well known to need elaboration here. It should suffice to say that, along with some others, Sanjay got a Letter of Intent from the Government to manufacture the 'small car'. This was to be priced at Rs. 8,000 so as to be within the reach of middle class people. The hike in price, however, would come later.

Enormous tracks of land for the factory—and to spare—were acquired in the neighbouring State of Haryana, just a few minutes' drive from Central Delhi. This became the basis of friendship between Sanjay and Bansi Lal, then the Chief Minister of Haryana, who was shrewd enough to see the political advantages of promoting the Prime Minister's son, and his car project. In the process of acquiring land, hundreds of villagers were callously dispossessed of their agricultural land. Besides, this land was very near defence installations, but who could question the Prime Minister's son who was also a friend of the Chief Minister?

The company shares sold like hot cakes. Every one wanted to be on the 'ground floor' of a Company in which the Prime Minister, through her son, was interested. It was not only the share capital which flowed in but also 'deposits' and 'guarantees' from would-be wholesalers and retailers. Quite a sizeable amount! Sanjay was, indeed, doing famously. It was capitalism without investing any capital of his own.

To sell cheap cars, you have first to manufacture them along an assembly line. The factory produced only eight or ten cars per week. It was not enough to meet the demand for the 'little car' which was already priced at four times its original price.

Where was he to get more money from? From nationalised banks, of course!

Now, in April 1974, the Prime Minister had gone out of her way to herself appoint a youngish man, Dharm Veer Taneja (50), as Chairman and Managing Director of the Central Bank of India. That he was a seniormost man available and that he had proved his competence as the Deputy General Manager of the same bank, was beside the point. The Prime Minister called him for advice on banking matters several times and once mentioned that she had full confidence in him as 'our man'. In his innocence, Taneja took this to imply that he was committed to a policy of nationalising banks for the good of the common man. That there was another meaning to the phrase 'our man' became apparent to him soon after.

When Taneja took charge he discovered (among other things) that the Central Bank had opened a branch in the Maruti factory premises near Gurgaon. Sanjay Gandhi had all along been approaching the Central Bank for funds through the Manager of the Branch as well as through the Zonal Manager in Delhi. Once or twice Taneja accompanied the bank officers to see the condition of the Maruti project and to examine the justification for further facilities. He found no worthwhile properties to justify a big loan.

One of the senior Maruti employees informed Taneja confidentially that during endurance tests for the car, the engine conked out on the way to the testing ground in Ahmednagar and had to replaced by an imported one.

Then came the climax. One day, Sanjay Gandhi made a pressing demand for funds for his small car project and the technical services. He wanted Rs. 2.5 crores, immediately.

While the proposal was being processed, Sanjay pressed Taneja for sanctioning an immediate loan for his consulting services. The conversation took place at the Prime Minister's house, and an officer of the bank accompanying Taneja witnessed Sanjay Gandhi venting his rage against the Chairman of the Central Bank. When the bank Chairman expressed his inability to sanction the loan, Sanjay threatened him not only with immediate dismissal but also physical liquidation.

Undaunted, the very next morning, Taneja issued written instructions to his zonal manager not to release any finance to Sanjay Gandhi. Taneja reported his action to the Reserve Bank of India and to the Banking Department of the Finance Ministry in the Government of India. They all concurred with him. C. Subramaniam, Finance Minister, told him that Maruti would be a mill-stone round the neck of the Congress Party at the next elections. This was said in January 1975 and it came true in March 1977!

Dharm Veer Taneja was an intellectual and a poet in his spare time. He recalled lines from his poem 'Nehru and Freedom':

What is that freedom about which I ask?
About freedom to starve and about freedom to die;
About freedom to suffer and about freedom to weep;
About freedom to wake and about freedom to sleep.
No, I ask not about these freedoms.
Such freedoms are not to us denied.
I fear not about the loss of these freedoms.
But I fear about the loss of personal freedom.
The freedom to laugh and the freedom to smile;
The freedom to grow and the freedom to decide;
The freedom to concede and the freedom to deny;
The freedom to be wrong and the freedom to be right;
The freedom to believe in truth and the freedom to
believe in lies.

He had not anticipated one other freedom—the freedom not to give loans to industrial upstarts. And now he was to pay the price for it.

On 23rd April 1975, Taneja was called to Delhi and orally informed that the Government had decided not to renew his term as Chairman. This was confirmed a little later in writing. The entire Board of Directors decided to protest to the Finance Minister but, curiously enough, he was not able to give them time (or was not allowed to) for an entire week. Then, one independent-minded public spirited Director of the bank, Romesh Thapar, resigned in protest against this kind of financial 'arm-twisting'.

A U.N.I. press report appeared in most of the newspapers on 30th May 1975:

A high level enquiry into the circumstances under which services of Central Bank Chairman, D.V. Taneja, were termina-ted was demanded by Jan Sangh leader, Atal Behari Vajpayee, at a public meeting at *Vaghodia* in Baroda District today. Mr. Vajpayee charged the Prime Minister, Indira Gandhi,

[14]

with sacking the Bank Chairman for not helping the Maruti Small Car project with an advance of Rs. 3.5 crores. He challenged Mrs. Gandhi to contest his allegation and declared that he was prepared to face the consequences.

The report was incorrect only in one unimportant detail. The amount asked for was not Rs. 3.5 crores, but Rs. 2.75 crores only!

While he could not make a small car, Sanjay Gandhi decided to build heavy truck bodies and steam-rollers. When he could not do that successfully he took over selling agencies of Piper airplanes and tractors, and started supplying them to State Governments that were only too willing to buy from the Prime Minister's son. On this, he or his Maruti factory got a fat commission.

Then he started 'consulting services' project to advise people on how to start, install and operate industries—all for a substantial 'consultation fee'!

At this stage, Finance Minister, C. Subramaniam, advised the young car manufacturer, to take the advice of K.K. Birla, the son of G.D. Birla, who had ample experience in manufacturing the Hindustan-Ambassador cars. So a meeting was arranged. No one knows what transpired at the meeting, but evidently Shri Birla imparted not only industrial know-how but also presented some of his economic ideas or ideology to the young man. How well Sanjay learnt this lesson was evident soon enough.

In August 1975, Sanjay Gandhi gave his first important interview to the editor of *Surge* in Delhi. This was, in a sense, the curtain-raiser for his debut on the stage of Indian politics. In this, Sanjay not only contradicted every idea and ideal of his grandfather, Jawaharlal Nehru, but practically repudiated (or some would say exposed) the allegedly progressive postures and policies of his own mother. Already, the pupil had learnt the lesson from his teacher. It was the 'voice of big business' in which the would-be big businessman or tycoon chose to speak.

Asked if he was in favour of nationalising any sector of the industry, he categorically said, "Not at all. Take coal. When coal was nationalised it was selling, I think, at 35 rupees a ton. They were making a profit. Now we are getting coal at about

90 rupees a ton and they are running a loss of 100 crores a year. The citizens are being made to pay 90 crores... they are also being made to pay for the loss of a 100 crores a year." (Big Business figures, Big Business arguments, very convincing, coming from the mouth of the son of the so-called socialist prime minister! And all in the name of the "citizens"!)

Asked to propose a panacea for all economic ills, he replied: "Well, one way is to remove blackmarketing. The best way is to lessen the tax. Suppose a person is earning a lot, O.K., you can say he is a nasty fellow and should not earn so much. But if he is earning it, he thinks he deserves to earn it. So he does not think he deserves to pay 95 per cent to the government...(or) over a 100 per cent of this income which means they were going into a loss."

Questioned further about the public sector and its functioning, Sanjay Gandhi, the grandson of Jawaharlal Nehru, replied: "I think public sector should function *only* in competition with the private sector.... where it cannot function in competition with the private sector, it should be allowed to die a natural death. Most of the private sector people... like Tatas, don't own Tatas, and Birlas, don't own Birlas. But the units have their names, they get these profits and they are happy, so it is O.K."

No president of the Federation of Chambers of Commerce could have improved on this manifesto. No wonder the Prime Minister, in his interest and her own, had to withdraw the statement in which her coalition colleagues, the Communists (i.e. C.P.I.), were squarely denounced as "corrupt". This politically embarrassed her though earlier she had already issued a statement against the Communists, calling them "traitors" to the national cause in 1942!

The important plank of *Sanjaywad* was that it did not believe in 'ism' or 'ideology', which was the hallmark of anti-communists and fascists everywhere.

Two months earlier, had come the Allahabad High Court judgement in which Indira Gandhi, while being found not guilty

on 50 counts, was held accountable on two technical charges.
One, engaging Yashpal Kapoor, a gazetted officer, as an electoral agent while his resignation had not been accepted; and the
other, allowing the state governments (not the Congress governments but the BLD!) to exceed a permissible height of the rostrum from which she spoke. These were merely technical grounds
which could hardly be called 'corrupt practices'. But technically,
and according to the letter of the law, they were such. She should
have resigned and then fought out the case in the Supreme Court.
Even some of her Congress Party supporters were advising her
to follow this course, which would have improved her image
as a law-abiding prime minister. For quite a while, Mrs. Gandhi
herself remained poised on the verge of a decision to resign.
Then something happened and it was all changed to—her detri-
ment, as events would prove later.

What exactly happened?
No one knows for certain. It is said that certain 'leftist' ele-
ments persuaded her to continue in office and defy the law.
Even the name of Moscow has been whispered in this connection.
We can only conjecture with the support of an eye-witness
account by Mrs. Subhadra Joshi.

Just when 'spontaneous' public sympathy was being expressed
by groups of scooter-drivers and rickshaw-pullers, Mrs. Joshi
found that some posters and sticking paste were being loaded in
a fleet of Ambassador cars under the supervision of a number of
young boys sitting on the lawns of 1 Akbar Road, the annexe to
the Prime Minister's house.

She asked what was going on and was told that it was an
arrangement to put up posters in support of the Prime Minister.
She was scandalised. Such self-publicity from the Prime Minister's
house would boomerang.

"Who has asked you to do this stupid thing?", she asked.

"Sanjayji", was the answer. "Sanjayji is looking after all
this", volunteered one of the boys.

And so 'Sanjayji' became the tactless, foolhardy custodian of his mother's political image.

But Subhadra Joshi, Member of Parliament, was made of sterner stuff. She telephoned Sanjay in the next bungalow and explained that, in the Prime Minister's interests, such a thing should not be done. Such activity showing solidarity with the Prime Minister would be better mobilised if organised from some other place than the residence of the person being supported. This had obviously not occurred to the foolish young man, who was impatient to do something to prove to his mother that he, and he alone, stood by her through thick and thin.

On 13th June, the next evening, somebody came to Subhadraji to say that there was a decision to stop electricity, water supply, and bus services in the city. This was allegedly to express the workers' solidarity with Indiraji and to demonstrate anger against the Allahabad judgement. This was in the middle of June, when Delhi was recording a temperature of 115 degrees Farenheit and above. Only a sadist could have thought of such measures. Subhadra Joshi was shocked. She immediately rang up the Lt. Governor. He confirmed the news, saying that orders to the contrary had to come from the Prime Minister herself.

As it was already late that night, Subhadra Joshi went to the Prime Minister's residence early next morning, without an appointment. She thought that some people were doing this without the Prime Minister's knowledge and that she should be informed before any damage was done. She told Mrs. Gandhi what she had heard and was shocked to find that Mrs. Gandhi was aware of it and had approved of the inhuman plot to roast the citizens of Delhi in summer without water. In vain did she plead for the people who would have to do without fans and without water in the June heat of Delhi.

Evidently, this had no effect on Indira, the daughter of Jawaharlal Nehru, whose father had believed in suffering with his people. Instead, Indira shouted back, "People do nothing and when we ourselves—I and *my son*—do something, they come to oppose and render pious advice."

Subhadra had not thought Indira capable of such inhumanity. Someone had convinced her that she must cling to power at all cost. Someone had 'sold' her this crazy scheme. Who? Sanjay, of course!

So Subhadra stood her ground, and also shouted back, and eventually Indira agreed to withdraw the scheme.

On 12th June 1975, as soon as Sanjay came to know the High Court judgement and that his mother was, on her own, contemplating resignation, he quickly computed his own assets and liabilities and came to one conclusion: she must not be allowed to abdicate the powers she held.

So, effacing any signs of calculating self-interest from his face, he became the affectionate son, concerned only with his mother's welfare.

"Amma", he purred softly in his nasal, effeminate voice, "You are *not* resigning!" That did it.

She was on the verge of a final decision. Her own inner convictions told her to resign and step aside for the interim period while the Supreme Court considered the appeal. Most of her ministers and advisers also approved of her resignation. This was the normal democratic thing to do. N.A. Palkhiwala, the eminent lawyer from Bombay, was contacted over the telephone and asked whether he would take up her case. He agreed and hoped to get a reversal of the Allahabad High Court judgement.

On the other hand, there was the problem of finding a suitable interim prime minister. Should it be Yeshwantrao Chavan? Or Jagjivan Ram? But supposing it was one of them; and he refused to step down in her favour after a favourable judgement?

Mrs. Gandhi knew well enough the corrupt and corroding effect of political power. Who wants to let go power once it is in hand? The other consideration was the political Opposition. Why were they clamouring for her immediate resignation when, even the High Court had given her three weeks' time? What was their game? Were they hoping to *hatao* Indira? If that was so, should she oblige them? She was in the depths of a dilemma when her second son, Sanjay, arrived and whispered to her, "Amma, you are not resigning. You will be playing your enemies' game. They would not get rid of you by hook or by crook! *You*

[19]

are not to resign, Amma. Understand?"

She understood. At that moment her mind was made up. When Palkhiwala arrived in Delhi and learnt of her decision not to step down while the case was being heard in the Supreme Court, he refused to take up the case. Otherwise, he was very hopeful that the two charges were too flimsy and technical to bear the scrutiny of the Supreme Court! But, on a matter of principle, he would take up the case only if she decided to step down.

"We have dozens of lawyers, Amma. Much bigger and better than Palkhiwala. He is a Swatantra man, any way! You cannot depend upon them."

So Mrs. Gandhi consulted H.R. Gokhale who was her minister in charge of law and judiciary.

Meanwhile, Sanjay started his hired publicity ballyhoo. His friend Bansi Lal, Chief Minister of neighbouring Haryana, gave him ample support by supplying truckloads of peasants from Haryana. They were promised five rupees per day plus the privilege of getting a *darshan* of the Prime Minister. What more could an agricultural wage-labourer expect?

So the people came, with bands playing, drums beating, Bhangra-dancers dancing; and they surrounded 1 Safdarjang Road, the Prime Minister's residence. Mrs. Gandhi knew it was all a stage-managed show, but when she went out she was under the illusion that the people really needed her. Of course, the crowds did include some who had sincerely come on their own—taxi-drivers and rickshaw-pullers who had benefited from bank nationalisation. The proportion was not more than that of salt in *khichri*, but she chose to mistake *khichri* for the salt.

They were men loyal to Sanjay and Bansi Lal, and therefore loyal to her—for the time being. For several days this show went on till the climax was reached at the Boat Club meeting—a spectacular show consisting of genuine supporters, those who had come out of curiosity as well as truckloads of peasants brought not only from Haryana but now, also from the neighbouring districts of Uttar Pradesh, the Punjab and Rajasthan.

A telephone call from Sanjay or even Dhawan, the Prime Minister's Additional Private Secretary, was enough to put the chief ministers on their feet. They vied with each other to send the maximum truckloads. Probably, all this was not spelt out in detail to Mrs. Gandhi; but she could not help seeing the line of trucks standing behind the crowds and know where they came from. She imagined that the people in their thousands had demonstrated their loyalty and affection for her, spontaneously!

This Boat Club meeting was, incidentally, the first public occasion when the entire family of the Prime Minister, including her grandchildren, was present on the dias. It was supposed to give a family atmosphere to the people fed on 'family melodramas'. But Sanjay was the most prominent and active of them all, and was heard making wisecracks at the expense of even the Congress Party President, Mr. D.K. Borooah.

The crowds stretched over a long distance and the people were so far away from the rostrum that from behind the microphones Mrs. Gandhi saw only a sea of faces, apparently admiring and idolatrous.

"*Amma*, didn't I tell you? You are not to believe others. You have to learn to trust only *me*—and the people!"

'And the people' had been added for effect. He meant that from now on he was to look after the interests of his mother. From that day, every day, Sanjay 'sold' the idea of 'emergency' to his mother. "*Amma*, this is an emergency. This so-called judicial judgement is all part of a conspiracy to push you out of power permanently. You must act at once."

This rally was not televised. Sanjay seized the opportunity. I.K. Gujral, then Minister for Information and Broadcasting, had said that it would be improper to televise this rally because it was only the Congress Party rally and not a government meeting. Mrs. Gandhi explained Gujral's viewpoint to Sanjay.

"He has a point there", she must have said.

"Nonsense, *Amma*!" Sanjay must have flared up. "Is he afraid of what the Opposition might say? He is not fit to be Minister for Information and Broadcasting."

The next morning Sanjay called for an explanation from Gujral. This was Sanjay's first assertion of extra-constitutional authority.

"I am answerable to the Prime Minister", Gujral answered, "not to her son!"

[21]

"All right, we shall see!"

There was a flicker of a smile—more a smirk—at the corners of Sanjay's lips. The fate of Gujral was sealed.

Next day, Sanjay had consultations with his friend, Bansi Lal, who suggested, "Why not have a smart and alert young man like Vidya Charan Shukla in place of that fellow Gujral. Gujral is a comic anyway. Send him to Moscow."

"*Amma*", said Sanjay playing his cards well at lunch time, "all my friends think that Gujral let you down very badly by not telecasting yesterday's huge public meeting."

"Do they?"

"Yes!", answered Sanjay, "they say it was the greatest public meeting ever held anywhere in the world."

"Yes, indeed! That is what I saw yesterday."

"He missed a great opportunity to show to the whole world how popular you are in India. It should have gone well on any TV in the world."

"Yes, I think it was a mistake on his part not to telecast it."

"*Amma*, you call it only a mistake? I would say: It is deliberate sabotage of a sensitive medium like TV. This should not be left in the hands of a man like Gujral, who may be a hidden man of the Opposition."

"Then, whom do you think...?"

That was the beginning.

"I think Vidya Charan Shukla should be transferred to the I. & B. Ministry.," said Sanjay.

And so within a few days, Shukla was the I. & B. Minister. Later, the 'comic' Gujral was packed off to India's embassy in Moscow.

Next day, came the Supreme Court judgment exonerating Indira Gandhi of "any of the grave electoral vices". The judgment said that she could continue as Prime Minister but would not have the right to vote in the Lok Sabha. There was no bar on her participation in parliamentary debates.

On 25th June the Opposition parties, mainly the Jana Sangh, which had powerful roots among the middle classes of Delhi, the Congress (O) and the Bharatiya Lok Dal, held a rally. It was a big meeting, though not as big as Mrs. Gandhi's. The Jana Sangh and RSS cadres had been mobilised not only from Delhi but from adjacent States and cities too.

It was at this meeting that Jayaprakash Narayan appealed to the police and the military to disobey any 'illegal' orders which did not conform to their conscience. Thus, unwittingly, Jayaprakash Narayan supplied Sanjay with the final argument in favour of proclaiming the emergency.

"*Amma*, did you hear that? They are asking the police and the army to revolt.! And you sit there, silent and unmoving. This is the clearest treason that would incite the soldiers to revolt."

The mother was already convinced of the need for declaring the emergency.

From now on Sanjay was to take more and more of the burden of the State off the shoulders of his mother. For this, she was grateful. He was her dutiful loyal son, wasn't he?

Special telephones were installed in the suite occupied by Sanjay Gandhi. R.K. Dhawan, the additional private secretary, was his ADC-in-waiting. With the advice of Bansi Lal, it was from this office that instructions were sent to police headquarters and to chief ministers of various states.

In the darkness of that night, the Opposition leaders were arrested and taken to their places of detention; they included Jayaprakash Narayan, who had once been described by Jawaharlal Nehru as "the future prime minister of India", and Morarji Desai, who had been Nehru's colleague for at least 30 years. That night was a 'black night' for the press, for most of the newspapers were deprived of the power to run their machines, under orders from Sanjay who was constantly on the telephone that night. Press censorship was also clamped down simultaneously.

Early next morning, Cabinet meeting was held at 1 Safdarjang Road. Sanjay was present, on his mother's invitation. Some thought it odd but no one said anything.

The proclamation of emergency was put before them for their

information, as though they were not her cabinet but only a
subservient body. The President had already been made to sign
the proclamation at midnight. Everyone thought discretion the
better part of valour and kept silent; except Swaran Singh who
asked softly and politely if the proclamation of emergency was
necessary. The meeting was only a formality and it was soon
time for the press to depart, since Mrs. Gandhi had to prepare
for nationwide radio broadcast.

Hardly had they left, when Sanjay whispered into his mother's
ears again:

"Did you hear what that Sardarji was saying? Is the emergency
necessary? *Amma*! In critical times like these, when your enemies
are asking the army Jawans to revolt against you, how can you
trust such a man to be your Defence Minister? You go and
finish your radio broadcast and come back. Then I'll tell you
the alternative."

She said that morning over the radio, that "a deep and wide-
spread conspiracy" was afoot, "since I began introducing certain
progressive measures of benefit to the common man of India."
(She had rejected Borooah's advice to announce some social
and economic reforms along with the emergency—proposals
vetoed outright by Sanjay.)

"Now we learn of new programmes, challenging law and
order throughout the country with a view to disrupting the normal
functioning of the government ... Duly elected governments have
not been allowed to function and, in some cases, force has been
used to coerce members to resign in order to dissolve lawfully
elected assemblies." (This happened to be true, but encouraging
'defection' was a game that Congress, in its time, had also played
to topple the Opposition ministries.)

She also referred to Jayaprakash Narayan's appeal to the
police and the army to disobey orders given by the authorities.
"How can any government worth the name stand by and allow
the country's stability to be imperilled?"

When his mother returned, Sanjay complimented her on her
performance. "It was very good", he said. "*Amma*, you deserve
a prize for that speech. Come into my room. Let me introduce
you to your next Defence Minister."

And thus Bansi Lal appeared on the scene and Indira was made to feel grateful to her son, who thought of everything—and did everything—without even asking her. He was indeed a doer and no talker!

3

❦

The Emergency

Q. "Don't you think you should have immediately gone
   there to Turkman Gate and to Khichdipur and other
   places where the people were then lying in the open
   and consoled them, if not begged their forgiveness?"
A. "No, I didn't go. That was a mistake on my part."

> Indira Gandhi in an interview with
> K.A. Abbas after Emergency was
> lifted and when she was not in
> power.

NOBODY CAN pinpoint what led to the declaration of the Emergency. But I know that, not knowing the extent of the displeasure
of the people over the Turkman Gate affair on the part of Indira
Gandhi must have been a factor.

So we have to go to the crux of the matter relating to Turkman
Gate. *Turkman Darwaja*, one of the many gates in the city wall
of the old Shahjehanabad—like *Ajmere* Gate, *Dilli darwaza* and
Kashmiri Gate and *Khooni darwaza*—is one of the landmarks
of Old Delhi.

The city wall, penetrated by a dozen or so gates, enclosed
one of the most congested parts of Delhi. Hindu and Sikh refugees from West Punjab were settled in the vacated empty houses
left behind by the Muslims who went on their own or were
driven out to Pakistan. But many Muslims had stayed on
at first putting up at Old Fort Muslim Refugee Camp and later

coming back at the time of Mahatma Gandhi's fast unto death. They were old Delhi merchants and craftsmen, some of whom had old styled houses. Some others were living in bigger *áeorhis* with marble verandahs (locally called *Da-laan*) made of marble and even had marble fountain in the inner courtyard. Other houses were occupied by the Hindu or Sikh refugees. It was thus a cosmopolitan area of Old Delhi and not an exclusively Muslim colony. It was congested but was, by no means, a slum. There was one stone-lined motorable central lane which emerged at the other end in the rear of the southern gate of the Jama Masjid with innumerable lanes and side lanes. Outside the city gate and the wall there was a cluster of huts (jhopdies) using the portion of the remaining wall to lean on. They were the houses of the homeless, including that of Jagdish Prasad, an old and white-haired employee of the Communist Party of India. He had made a pucca house to accomodate his family with bricks which distinguished a house from a hut. He had put in a regular door. All these did not look like a slum which had to come under the huge bulldozer.

All these *pucca* or *kachcha* houses were the first to be bulldozered. Jagdish Prasad had to beg his employers for another loan to hire a truck to take him to the new land, Khichdipur, three miles beyond the Jamuna Bridge. This was wilderness where all the derelicts had been dumped aptly called Khichdipur.

This, then, was the strategem of the new Shahjehan with the assistance of the legal authority of Deputy Governor of Delhi, Jagmohan. Jagmohan had a flair for writing and had only a few days earlier written a book on old Delhi, under Sanjay's instructions, suggesting demolition of the Hindu-Muslim dwellings along the side of the Turkman Gate. His master plan included the construction of a road which would start from the square in front of the Assembly Chamber of New Delhi straight to Jama Masjid thus linking Old and New Delhi. This was an attempt to redesign the twin cities. Jagmohan was on record as being in love with Old Delhi, including the congested area. One day, while talking to Sanjay Gandhi about his dream of beautifying Delhi and New Delhi and connecting Turkman Gate with New Delhi, Jag Mohan presented his book about Delhi to Sanjay Gandhi.

Without reading the book, Sanjay Gandhi declared, "I don't want dreamers, I did not ask you to give me a lecture on your dreams. I am a doer, and I like doers. I want you to clean up this dirty and damned old city".

Jagmohan wanted to be the Chairman of the Delhi Development Authority. Here was his opportunity if only he did exactly what Sanjay Gandhi wanted him to do. So he promised Sanjay, "I promise you, within three months". But the doer-in-a-hurry wanted it done in a week even quicker. The young man said, "Don't you know there is an Emergency on?" Jagmohan pleaded that it will be done in a hurry, "After all it won't be possible for all the people to leave the place to allow the demolition of their houses . . . . . . "

"Haven't you heard of bulldozers", Sanjay queried.

And so the bulldozers arrived, as if by magic, to bull-doze Turkman Gate and all the huts and houses within and outside the wall.

While the bulldozers were razing the Turkman Gate and the buildings within it and also outside, the people were dumped into trucks which then went straight across the Jamuna to the wilderness which would be called Khichdipur in the course of time. Hoardings were put up there promising (on paper) all the amenities of a civilized life. One such board, which I saw standing in the midst of Khichdipur, on March 21, 1977, nineteen months later, read as follows:

DELHI DEVELOPMENT AUTHORITY

Facilities Provided

Plots 11,440
Primary Schools 4
Nursery Schools 2
Higher Secondary School 1
Literary Centres 2

Dispensary 1
Parks 32
Local Shopping Centres 4
Convenient Shopping Centres 3
Milk Booths 2
Post Offices 2
Hand Pumps 410
Hydrants 112
Dust Bins 25
Lavatory Seats 1,504
Work Centres 4
Roads 150 kilometres
Lanes 20 kilometres
Tube Wells 5

Shaikh Abdullah, who happened to be in Delhi at that time, accompanied by a man who had come from Khichdipur, went to the sight of demolition at Turkman Gate. The Shaikh saw signs of destruction, then went to Khichdipur, the new abode of the bulldozed common people, and listened to their complaints to be conveyed to Indira Gandhi. The man accompanying him, was arrested by the Police on some trumped-up charge but the Shaikh insisted that he would not leave without him. Only then he was released.

I had welcomed Emergency in the beginning for I thought it would discipline the nation. But soon I was involved in an incident.

I had a strange personal experience of censorship, which unwittingly revealed Sanjay's hand in the Turkman Gate affair. On a visit to Delhi in July 1975, I heard of the sad case of a working woman uprooted from Turkman Gate. She used to bring her two children to the household where she worked as a maidservant. When asked as to why she brought them along, she explained that their *jhuggi* had been destroyed by the bulldozer and that they had been sent off to a distant, low-lying place which was water-logged. The rains brought with it a new menace—slithering cobras and pythons which were dangerous to the dwellers, some of whom had died of snakebite. Knowing nothing about

Sanjay Gandhi's hand in it, I attributed this unfortunate story. "to bureaucratic cruelty and callousness".

The censor returned the article saying orally that "the Delhi clean-up campaign was Sanjay Gandhi's department and so no adverse remarks about it would be tolerated". I re-wrote the piece as a second feature two weeks later, underplaying it a little, and attributing the reason to "bureaucratic ineptitude" without mentioning Sanjay Gandhi, it got through with the words intact: "For these 'new refugees' who have been thrown out, away, from Delhi, the old adage gets a new meaning: *Hanooz Dilli door ast!*" (Still Delhi—the promised land—is far off!),

Shaikh Abdullah, in an interview with me later in Srinagar, said: "Turkman Gate was nothing but a symbol of the arrogance of Power". This cost Indira Gandhi her seat in Parliament.

The Shaikh's visit had a sequel. A deputation met the Prime Minister under the leadership of Bashiruddin Shafi. After waiting for two hours they were informed that the Prime Minister could not meet them. As was usual, she referred them to Sanjay. He asked them to turn informers and give the names of all those who had defied the police. (Even after arresting 622 persons, including more than 50 children, he was not satisfied!) Besides that, he told them tauntingly: "Go to Shaikh Abdullah! He will come to your rescue". Then he made them an offer. "Write a letter to Shaikh Abdullah and tell him that all you told him were lies!" The deputation returned empty-handed, but with anger and hatred in their hearts.

More and more people were being disillusioned with the Emergency. I found that the Emergency Censors were playing ducks and drakes with my creative works in Urdu. No wonder more and more intellectuals were revising their opinion of the Emergency.

Loopholes in the Emergency were becoming manholes.

Inder Mohan, the social worker whom I had met in Delhi Coffee House, was awakened at 1 a.m. and arrested for no reason except that he had (as usual) drafted a memorandum for the Muslim refugees of the Turkman Gate. He had an audience with Sanjay Gandhi which did not go well. Sanjay asked him to produce some crores of rupees. That was Sanjay's idea of humour.

That night, he heard a knock on the door an hour past midnight. He was taken in preventive custody and put in a small room, along with hardened criminals. There was a receptacle put in one corner. Inder Mohan got his share of beating by the goondas, and though he shouted for help no policeman came to his rescue. This 'punishment' was the favourite gambit of the Delhi Police under the British Raj. What was then applied to Congressmen was now being done in the name of Congressmen and by the Congressmen to those who provoked that crooked smile of Sanjay Gandhi. Yet, Inder Mohan was not an unknown politician. He was a very well known social worker, a refugee from the partitioned Punjab. He was known to the Prime Minister Indira Gandhi. He himself knew several junior ministers and ex-ministers like Inder Kumar Gujral (who was now sent to Moscow as an Ambassador). This was tantamount to sending some Russian to Siberia as punishment but Gujral welcomed the opportunity.

There were many types of prisoners during the Emergency: first, there were the leaders—Charan Singh, Morarji Desai and some more who were given no pain, but had their movements restricted within some rest house or dak bungalow which was technically assumed to be a prison under a Police guard. Probably, they got some much needed rest and time enough to plan their next strategy. Jayaprakash Narayan was, while the Emergency lasted, mostly in one hospital or another. Now, he was physically unfit for those exercises of climbing the walls and running out of jail. He was too ill and infirm to repeat the 'Quit India' drama of jailbreak.

The junior leaders and newspapermen who were involved in Baroda Dynamite Case were roughly treated in Tihar Jail or earlier in the Hissar jail in Haryana. 'Dynamite being used by revolutionaries to derail goods trains so that transport would be blocked and yet there would be minimum (or none) human suffering. This was a new concept of non-violence. George Fernandes testified in a statement to the court and recounted how his family was treated:

My brother, Lawrence Fernandes, was arrested on May 1,

1976 in Bangalore. He was brutally tortured for 15 days, his bones fractured, his teeth broken. He was starved, denied even drinking water, and was reduced to a physical and nervous wreck. He is still in prison. His only offence is that he refused to disclose my whereabouts to the police. My younger brother Michael, is in detention under MISA for over 13 months now. My wife and three-year-old son are in exile, but fighting.

As for the lowest members of the opposition parties it was the same experience the Congressmen had once undergone. The police were still the same but the Police Ministers were now different.

On the recommendation of Sanjay Gandhi, Bansilal was made the Minister for Defence in the Central Government. It was but natural that the new Defence Minister obliged his patron by the lucrative contracts to supply trucks and other defence equipments ordered from USA and West Germany. All this was done in the name of Maruti Enterprises, which was the private limited Company started by Sanjay Gandhi. Unfortunately for Bansilal and Sanjay, the Emergency ended so soon.

There is enough evidence of excesses in the Family Planning Programme. The District Magistrates were given quotas of men and women who were to be sterilised. Not all the sterilizations were performed with due care, nor in hygienically perfect conditions. The police was often used to 'persuade' the ignorant women and men. They fulfilled their quotas by the use of *Danda* and the *goli* (bullet). Many excesses were committed. May be some good was achieved by reducing the population growth. At a road-side tea-shop in Uttar Pradesh I met an illiterate villager. He told me how he was forcibly sterilized when caught by the police. But, afterwards, the Man was quite satisfied with the operation.

While the late Indira Gandhi must take maximum responsibility for the excesses of this Emergency, she must also be given due credit to have decided to order the democratic elections, to abide by its results which did not go in her favour and to end the Emergency.

Indeed, 20th March, 1977 was the death-knell of Emergency, the democratic processes which she had ordered to be in abeyance had to be restored.

There was one of the peculiar qualities of this Emergency. It was practically invisible. Only one percent of the population saw it—the newspaper editors, or those who were in the Opposition party. The ordinary citizen got tickets for train, bus or aeroplane without paying any premium. Likewise, the Black market for cinema tickets was now in the doldrums. The operators of the Black Market were behind bars under the Emergency Laws.

The tourists who came from abroad, were amazed to see that there were no visible signs of the Emergency. They had read in the newspapers and news magazines about the Emergency (which they took to be some form of Martial Law). There was hardly any sign of Police or Army anywhere in the cities or the major cities on their itinerary. The midnight knock on the door was a phenomenon which was not carried out every day or everywhere.

A friend of mine from France, a mature diplomat and her husband, a teacher of European History in Brussels, were disappointed not to see any signs of Emergency in the streets of Bombay or at the tourist spots in Rajasthan and Kashmir. Every night she expected "knock on her door". But the policemen were extra polite to foreigners and the hotel employees never knocked except to remind the passengers of the early morning flight to take them across this large country.

"Where can I see the Emergency?" she asked me.

I told her that if she wanted to know about the Emergency she had to contact the opposition parties, or better still, the smugglers and the dealers in Black Money and foreign exchange. Or, if she went to Bangalore, she could try to contact Snehlata Reddy, a lady of rare accomplishments who was arrested on 1st May 1976 only because she knew the underground leader George Fernandes, socially. She was continually interrogated about the activities of the underground including whereabouts of George Fernandes. She was arrested and detained in a dingy solitary cell in Bangalore 'Maximum security' prison. She was a victim of asthma, very near the end of her life; they released her. Within a few months she was dead and all the screen weeklies carried the news of her death and wrote long obituaries. They wrote about her first film—*Samskara*—that won film forum's prize for

[33]

a director's first film, and went on to win the President's Gold Medal for being the best picture of the year. Meanwhile, along the opposition grapevine and according to the underground cyclostyled bulletins, many sensitive persons were being tortured in prison cells?

Transferred to Tihar Central Jail, the infamous prison in Delhi, George Fernandes was further consoled by a small transistor radio which was presented to him, on which he could hear the songs from Indian films.

The results of 1977 General Elections were coming in now even on George's transistor radio. The Congress suffered a land-slide defeat, except in some Southern states.

The security guards became somewhat friendlier to George, when they were fitting handcuffs and fetters on his hands and feet, mumbling "it's being done for the last time" as they were taking him to the *Tis Hazari* Court.

The results being broadcast by All India Radio and duly scrib-bled on big black boards in prominent places in Delhi and New Delhi, were also heard on the big sized radio of Madame Rukhsana Singh, in a small house in Central Delhi. Every defeat of the Congress was a direct slap in her face. But she was sad that even some of their closest friends and supporters had lost the election. What will they do without their friends in parlia-ment? While listening to the radio she ordered her maidservant: *"kapada nikalo. Ek dam jaldi-jaldi"*.

The maid-servant brought a resplendent red and gold sari.

But what will Madame say to this? "These bright clothes as if I was enjoying and celebrating the failure of her party men?"

But in the personal wardrobe of Rukhsana was a white *shal-war qamees* suit with a white *dopatta*.

"This is better;" (her heart warned) "better we prepare." She would normally wear white not to look ostentatious on this day. Better keep a black *odhnie* also. Black is for any tragedy.

The same afternoon she presented herself at the Family Planning office near Jama Masjid. But there was no sign of Sanjay's limousine here.

She dialled Sanjay's private number at his home. A minor minion responded. Recognizing her voice and tone, he informed her, *"Saheb to Amethi aur Rae Bareilli gaye hain. Brahmachariji ke saath. Hawai jehaz mein . . . Sham tak aaengay.".* (Sahib is gone to Amethi and Rai Bareilli with Brahmachariji in a special aeroplane; will return in the evening.)

"Aur kya khabren hain?" she asked unnecessarily

"Khabren to radio par bohat kharaab aa rahee hain." And he put down the phone.

Indira Gandhi mastered the difficult art of not reacting to the adverse news. But the news of staunch supporters' failures was too much for her to bear. She switched off her radio.

But in Sanjay's apartment and the Secretaries' Room the A.I.R. news, that was Voice of History, was muffled by the distance. Yet she could still hear it.

"So-and-so of Janata Party has an enormous lead over his Congress rival . . . . "

She closed the bedroom door and lay down on her bed. However she might try to muffle it, the Voice of History kept up its drone. Now she knew her own fate!

4

The Enemy Strikes

"Only the friend warns. The enemy strikes!"

> —The last words of my book, *That Woman*, published in 1977, which were taken from the beginning of my LAST PAGE of 19th February, 1977, weeks before the Election results came out.

THE EMERGENCY. It was ended as it was begun by Indira Gandhi. Even in January 1977, it was petering out. The elections were announced and the Press Censorship was much more liberal now. I was allowed to write on the LAST PAGE an article headed— I BEG YOUR PARDON, MADAM.

Now I could give facts and figures of the 'Emergency' arrests and detentions which totalled upto 64,000 men and women, including Durga Bhagwat, the widely respected intellectual and President of the Marathi Sahitya Sammelan. She was jailed for a speech she had delivered to the students of a Bombay college.

The *Seminar*, a monthly edited by the progressive intellectual, Romesh Thapar, who was not long ago reputed to be a member of the Kitchen Cabinet of Indira Gandhi, had closed down his journal rather than submit to the indignity of Press Censorship.

The attitude of *Mainstream* was similar.

Even the *Patriot*, which was the friendliest and the least critical of all the dailies published from Delhi, was given a hint to be submissive by the stoppage of Government advertisements.

The Emergency was supported by the capitalists. During the Emergency, strikes and agitations for higher wages and bonus were banned. In effect, the Government was not neutral in the disputes between the mill-owners and the labour. The abolition of 'bonded labour' was merely an eye-wash. This was revealed in a series of articles by Dileep Padgaonkar in *The Times of India*. Many of the poor slaves believed that they were still living in the *Raj* of the Company Bahadur! The Prime Minister Indira Gandhi had often spoken on the theme of 'Grow More Trees'. But, her Government had no scruples about giving a contract to the Birlas to cut millions of trees in Kerala and Kashmir.

As regards the Prime Minister's 20 Points (which was supposed to outline the revolutionary economic programme), it became soon clear that they were given for implementation to a frankly anti-revolutionary bureaucracy.

I concluded the LAST PAGE (19th February 1977) with the words: "This is both an assessment—and a warning!"

On 2nd April, I noted in the LAST PAGE:

The Emergency was liked by—

—the taxi-drivers and scooter-drivers whose dream of owning their own vehicles was fulfilled because of the nationalised banks giving them loans to buy their own vehicles with reasonable (not *Sahukari*) rates of interest.

—the poor *agarbatti*-seller who used to do his petty business by borrowing money from the *Sahukars* on 10 per cent interest *per month*, who was persuaded to go to a Bank and borrow money (only Rs. 500) on 12 per cent interest *per year*, repayable in instalments, and he had repaid it in full in less than six months, and now he is the master of his own little business.

—the poor students who could get their expensive books free from the Book Bank in their college, and note books at subsidised rates.

—the backward tribal students (specially girls) who were getting free education in their *ashrams*.

[37]

—the tribal women of Mandla district who have got back their silver jewellery because of the moratorium on rural debts, and the prompt action taken by an exceptionally imaginative and humane young Collector.

A crowd had gathered in the morning light at Gandhiji's Samadhi at Raj Ghat. Most of the faces were unfamiliar. The few familiar faces were those of the leaders. They included the drawn shaved face of Jayaprakash Narain, the 81-year-old shining face of Morarji Desai, and the lean and angular face of Acharya J.B. Kripalani. There was also the dark and bulky figure of Babu Jagjivan Ram, the chubby face of Atal Behari Vajpayee with the lean and thin L.K. Advani, former editor of the Jana Sangh weekly *The Organizer*, close behind. And lastly, the unfamiliar but youthful black-bearded face of Prakash Singh Badal with his rosy cheeks of the Punjab. The mass of unfamiliar faces were those of the newly elected Janata Party M.Ps. They bore self-confident smiles, as if that was enough to admit them into the hitherto unknown precincts of the Lok Sabha for their swearing-in session. They were happy as they had defeated the old fogies of the Congress and brought about a 'Revolution' in India—by ballots and not by bullets'! But they did not know that to govern what was required was some experience, some aplomb and at least some tradition.

The Pledge, which was haltingly read out by the infirm and obviously ill Jayaprakash Narain (who was seated on a wheel-chair), was translated into English for the sake of the few South Indians who were conspicuous in the gathering by their small number.

Jayaprakash's voice was feeble as a resut of his long illness. Very few, other than those in the front row, were able to follow him or his words. But they knew that it was on their behalf that he was reading out the Pledge. It was a pledge to serve the people, the *Janata*, without fear or favour. But common people of India did not, at first, know the meaning of Democracy. But they had learnt it from their sons and daughters.

After this, they dispersed by various means of transport ranging from buses to limousines.

This was to be their Finest Hour. But they were all hungry for breakfast. From tomorrow, they would not have to worry about it. The canteen in the Parliament House would serve them hot and spicy meals.

The Morarji Desai Cabinet took charge of the country a few days before the 1st of April, which was All Fools' Day!

Nowhere Morarji Desai had been an important Minister, not long ago, until he differed with Indira Gandhi over the Government's economic policy. Now he had become the head of the Government.

But for Atal Behari Vajpayee, it was his first experience of entering the South Block.

Indira Gandhi shifted her dwellings from the small bungalow on Akbar Road to the bungalow of her friend, Mohammed Yunus, at Willingdon Crescent. This was a comfortable enough place. But she still had to provide for the crowds of people who, even now, came to see her from all over India. The old official staff was given leave, but her personal Secretariat was kept intact. She was now relieved of Prime Ministerial responsibilities. She was not even a Member of Parliament. But her hours of work would continue to be the same.

Interviewed by me, on March 5, 1978, she said that she felt as if a big load had been taken off her shoulders. She was relieved of a heavy load of work, but she was still the Head of the Congress Party. She had now more time to study and for reading books which she had bought or which had been presented to her.

She woke up early and went to bed late. She divided her time between her sons, grandchildren, and friends who called upon her more freely now.

5

❀

A Drama in Four Acts

INDIRA GANDHI was summoned to Court.

Policemen—the very same Policemen who worked for the Emergency—came to her house and served the summons. She had been expecting them, and when they arrived, she offered them tea while they waited. She read the long summons and only then did she sign. This is how the 'Last Page reported the event.

I

'Where is Indira Gandhi?'

'She had been arrested in Delhi.'

'Where were they taking her?'

'They were taking her to Bhatkal Dak Bungalow in Haryana, where she had imprisoned some of the top Janata leaders!

'Why did they not take her to Bhatkal?'

'Her lawyer said the warrant was issued by a Delhi Court, and they could not take her to Haryana! So they stopped at the Haryana border.'

II

'Where did she spend the night?'

'She spent the night in a Gazetted Officers' Hostel in Delhi. That was managed by the Home Ministry.'

'How did she sleep?'

'She slept very well—*As usual*, she said.'

[40]

'Did she get breakfast?'
'Yes—she took some fruit.'
'Inciuding the 'Forbidden Fruit'?'
'I don't know about that!'
'If she had to be taken to a Gazetted Officers' Hostel, why was she not allowed to sleep in her own bed?'
'I can't answer that. Ask the Home Minister Charan Singh!'
'Where is Indira Gandhi?'
'She is in Court where she has been taken through demonstrating crowds of her admirers and her critics.'

III

'Where is Shri Charan Singh?'
'He is addressing a Press Conference.'
'What is he saying?'
'He is explaining why it was necessary to arrest Mrs. Indira Gandhi.'
'And where is Mrs. Gandhi?'
'She is sitting at home, giving an interview to correspondents.'
'But she was arrested.'
'That was yesterday.'
'What happened today?'
'Today she was freed by Court as there was not sufficient *prima facie* evidence to arrest her.'
'Where is she going now?'
'She is going to Bombay on the way to Gujarat—according to her previous plan!'

IV

'Why this crowd at Santa Cruz airport today?'
'Indira Gandhi is coming from Delhi and going on to Gujarat.'
'But why this enormous crowd?'
'Thanks to Home Minister Charan Singh—because she was arrested yesterday.'
'Who arranged all the flowers and the trucks to bring the people in?'

[41]

'The Maharashtra Congress—and the Government.'

'What is she doing now?'

'She is addressing the gathering.'

'What is she saying?'

'She is saying that the Janata Government arrested her as a part of its political vendetta!'

'Is it true?'

'Could be—that's what the American press is also saying!'

'What are the people shouting?'

'They are saying *Indira Gandhi Zindabad—Charan Singh Murdabad*'!

'Where is she sleeping tonight?'

'In the V.I.P. lounge.'

'Why not in the Centaur Hotel, just across the road! It would have been more comfortable.'

'Probably she can't afford it!—Or perhaps she feels that the V.I.P. lounge is good enough for her. After all, she is going away in the morning.'

'Where is she going? So early in the morning?'

'She is going to Gujarat by car along the Highway.'

'What are these arches?'

'They have been put up by the villagers and tribals to welcome 'Indira Gandhi.'

'What is she saying to them?'

'In her ten minutes speech she is saying that she is going to return to politics to serve the people.'

'Will she, really?'

'I don't know, but she might.'

'Was it a good tour?

'Yes—very good! Crowds all the way! And a big meeting at the end of it in Bulsar.'

[42]

'Why Bulsar?'
'She wanted to storm the constituency of Morarji Desai.'
'That she did!'
'Now she is back in Delhi at 12, Willingdon Crescent.'
'When will the drama be repeated?'
'When God—or Home Minister Charan Singh—wills it!'

6

❀

A Creaky Government

"Mourn not the dead,
"But rather honour the pathetic throng,
"Who are the world's anguish and the wrong,
"But dare not speak."

—Ralph Chaplin, one of America's
poets whose verses Indira Gandhi
is fond of.

INDIRA GANDHI, though now out of power was keenly watching
the signs of cracking in the Janata Ministry. The Janata Party had
been a year old and was already showing lack of stability. The
Charan Singh-Morarji Desai feud was boiling over and the rift
within the party was widening.

Delhi was full with rumours. Both parties were mobilizing
support. One even heard that Morarji Desai was bent on remov-
ing the veteran Choudhary Saheb from the Home Ministership.
He was thinking of entrusting an enlarged agriculture Ministry
to Charan Singh. This could be poetic justice of some sort since
the Choudhary Saheb had been loudly blaming Nehru for negle-
cting agriculture. This, even though the over-all agricultural
production had improved, in fact almost doubled, with Punjab
becoming one of the most prosperous of states.

As many as ninety members of the Janata Party in Parliament
defied the party mandate and absented themselves when voting
on the Constitution Amendment Bill was taking place.

The Morarji Desai-Charan Singh differences was not the

only feud within the Janata Party. Also the Morarji Desai-George Fernandes feud which arose from their different approaches to the Maharashtra Government Employees' strike. Morarji Desai took a stand supporting Vasant Dada Patil's attitude, which defied 90,000 strikers, while George Fernandes supported the strikers. A new dimension was given to these different attitudes by the multi-nationals who lent a hand in widening the breach. George was accused of partiality towards a West German firm. The charge was made by another multi-national computing firm.

The hopes (or illusions) that the success of the Janata Party in March 1977 elections had raised were dispelled. The Janata wave was receding. "Janata Will Lose" was the headline in a popular Bombay weekly. Even I predicted in the next election not more than thirty per cent would vote for the Janata Party.

In Ahmedabad, a Yajna incurring an expense of a crore of rupees was held while millions of poor people of Gujarat starved. At a time when pure *ghee* was unavailable for even life-saving Ayurvedic medicines, thirty thousand kilograms of pure *ghee* was fed to the flames of the Yajna. Fifty thousand litres of milk was poured into the fire while babies were weeping and howling for a half bottle of milk. While the poor were starved for the lack of a few grains of rice, 250 quintals of rice and oil-seeds were consumed by the fire of this Yajna.

While people—mostly rationalists and agnostics—were sore about the spectacle of Brahmachari's sandals clattering over the corridors of the late Prime Minister's House, the Janata regime was no less involved with *tantriks*, *Swamis*, *Yogis* and the practitioners of religious mumbo-jumbos.

Railway pass was given to a *tantrik* to travel with his wife; he was caught misusing the pass in a coupe with some other young woman. Trunk calls to Raj Narain in the Lok Sabha premises were made by this *tantrik* and on his intervention the whole matter was suppressed.

The Yajna was inaugurated by a Maharani (Rajmata of Baroda) and presided over by a Shankaracharya. The inspiration came from the famous Jaigurudev, the big election time supporter of the Janata Party. He was one of the arrested persons under the Emergency for impersonating Netaji Subhash Chandra Bose at Kanpur. His 25-lakhs *Satyug Aagman Mahayajna* was the curtain raiser for the 3-crore Mahayajna of Ahmedabad.

The only ray of hope was the action of the young men of Ahmedabad, mostly students who were members of the former Nav Nirman Samiti, who received support from other organisations. They held a parallel Yajna, where Corruption, Bribery, Superstitions and Fascism were consigned to the flames. Speeches and lectures where held and pictorial posters were put up to educate the populace.

Meanwhile, four diseases had struck Bombay and Maharashtra —*Bombay Fever*, Typhoid and Jaundice, and the fourth one was Election Fever which was raging in the city and the states. Yet it was the minority voters who were uncontaminated. They were non-committal about the issues involved in the Elections.

There were two Congresses—Reddy (K. Brahmanand) and Indira Gandhi—which were united just a few months earlier. There was the Janata Party, here too there was hardly any perceptible difference in terms of unity. The voters saw that the Janata Party was engaged in a series of squabbles.

The disillusionment was more acute where the *Sahukari* system prevailed, because, many hopes had been reposed on the new Government at the time of March 1977 election. Scenes of extra-constitutional authority and personal rivalry began appearing on the surface. The peoples needs and requirements were neglected. The odour of corruption could be smelt again. The fancies of men in power like prohibition were being paraded to the neglect of the people's genuine needs and demands.

The one crore Yajna held in Ahmedabad was patronized by Janata followers. But the people knew that the former rulers of the Congress were not less prone to superstitions. But to this was now added the revivalism of the Rashtriya Swayam Sevak Sangh, the fanaticism of the erstwhile Jan Sangh and the authority of the Janata Party rulers.

In U.P and Bihar, this revivalism started taking a dangerous turn. A statue which was unveiled by the Janata Defence Minister Babu Jagjivan Ram was purified: thus even distinguished Harijan was being insulted. In the villages dominated by the upper castes,

Harijans were being shot or burnt alive. Was it a new inter-caste hostility? Such sadism and violence is something new. The Harijans are landless labourers while upper caste peasants have become *kulaks*. The oppressed class was becoming conscious of its rights and status granted under the Constitution. The Communists—specially the Naxalites—were making them class-conscious and better informed about their rights. The kind of assertiveness expressed by Harijans is what led to pogroms and mass murders conducted by the upper castes. Indira Gandhi appeared to the Harijans as their only saviour.

This was a God-sent opportunity for Indira Gandhi. Under the influence of Mahatma Gandhi and her father Jawaharlal Nehru she had no faith in untouchability and had genuine sympathy for the Harijans. Besides she was also a shrewd politician and knew when and how to project herself as a sympathiser of Harijans. The zamindars' cruelty to Harijans had reached such proportions that entire colonies of Harijans were burning. When she got to know about the case of arson and murder in the remote village of *Belchi* in Bihar, she left her air-conditioned bungalow and flew to the nearest airport. There she got into a car. The last ten miles or so were the most difficult and she had to complete the last lap of the journey by mounting an elephant and riding through the swamp. She was there even before the reporters. Dismounting from her high perch she talked to the Harijans. She reminded them about their constitutional rights they were not to forgo. The burning huts were still smouldering while the poor Harijans cheered and adored her as a goddess who rode an elephant and came through a slush to reach them.

This was, what is known in newspaper parlance, "Investigative Reporting". She came back and did not hide even from the press in India and the world. She told the grim story at the press conference. This was more than what Janata ministers had done. The three elders (Morarji Desai, Chaudhari Charan Singh, Jagjivan Ram) were too old to do it: the others were indifferent. They did not realise that by her visit to the charred remains of Belchi she had assured for her party millions of Harijan votes all over the country in the next elections. Reporting was, in the language of journalism, a "scoop" and also it was a political exposure which would cost leaders who misnamed the party as the Janata Party dearly in the next elections.

In all parties defections were chronic. The phenomenon of "Aya Ram-Gaya Ram" was being repeated. With a secret smile Indira Gandhi was quietly watching the "democratic" Janata's plight. They made the great blunder in making Morarji Desai Prime Minister, she thought. They made the same mistake that the 'Syndicate' of elder Congressmen had made by agreeing to make Indira Gandhi, prime minister in 1966, hoping that she would remain a 'goongi gudiya' (dumb doll). She did not remain so. Likewise with Morarji Desai. People like Choudhary Charan Singh had hope that the seemingly pliant Morarjibhai would take action after ascertaining the opinions of other elders. They were now surely disappointed. Morarji Desai believed in the God-like infallibility of his judgement—he never made a mistake. The alliance of two such characters was impractical. Morarji realised that he had made only one mistake—that of appointing Charan Singh as his Home Minister!

Another enigmatic 'smile' lighted up the face of Indira Gandhi when George Fernandes revealed in the Lok Sabha that a certain businessman from Bombay had been offered 20 lakhs for buying over the members of the legislatures (Congress or Janata?).

Two Forward Bloc members shouted for C.I.D. enquiry into the affair. The speaker could restore order amidst the pandemonium that was raised only with great difficulty. Three questions were raised:

1. Who had twenty lakhs (of BLACK MONEY, of course) to bribe the legislators?
2. To which political party did the might-have-been legislators belong? To Congress (I) or Janata? Or to both?
3. Which party was baiting these legislators? What is the current price of the legislators in the Aya Ram or Gaya Ram market?

The little dusty town of Chikmagalur in Karnataka will go down in contemporary history as the place which gave the political 'face' to Indira Gandhi. She won the by-election from Chik-magalur against the Janata candidate Virendra Patil by a wide margin in this southern town. She returned to the Lok Sabha as the Honourable Member from Chikmagalur. This, despite the nearby coffee estates. These were owned by capitalists and the owners tried to resist Indira Gandhi in a way which swept off the Janata on the one hand, and the Congress on the other, off their feet.

Chikmagalur was a bad omen and danger-signal to the already cracking Janata party, and its rule.

At the last elections, Rae Bareili had spelt the doom of an incipient dictatorship of Indira Gandhi (or her son Sanjay). It was a vote in favour of Raj Narain—many of the voters had never heard of him. Nor knew of his ideas. They did not even care whether he had any ideology at all. The vote was against Indira Gandhi and against the real or imagined excesses of the Emergency imposed by her. Most certainly, it was the Emergency that ensured the defeat of Indira Gandhi in 1977.

People are concerned with the crux, the basic and the ultimate truth of any situation. In Rae Bareili it was the issue of compulsory sterilizations of thousands. They were not concerned with the accomplishments or the distortions of this truth. They focused their mind's telescope on the centre of the problems, and ignored all that lay on the periphery. All this was true with the people of Chikmagalur. The voters, various segments of them, were concerned with economic and social problems. The Harijans were protesting against the atrocities by the upper classes and the higher (economic or social) castes, since the Janata Party had assumed power.*

The poor, including the landless labourers, were protesting against the pro-kulak policies and programmes of the Janata

*A total of 3,240 cases of violence against the Harijans were reported from all over India, in just six months (March 77 to September 77). This was stated by the Home Minister in Rajya Sabha. Over a hundred Harijans were murdered in Madhya Pradesh alone, said a Bhopal report.

The crime graph shows that thefts have increased in Delhi from 1,300 in 1976 to 2,700 in 1977; Kidnapping from 1,578 to 2,600; murders from 120 to 180; rapes from 40 to 70 and dacoities from 5 to 17.

regime, specially the policies of Choudhary Charan Singh's group.

The intelligentsia too was disillusioned with the negative record of the Janata leadership. Communal riots were unknown in South India. They happened far away in North and Central India which are the strongholds of R.S.S. Pernamba in Tamil Nadu and Adoni in Andhra Pradesh are two typical towns where inter-communal feuds were absent. The Hindu-Muslim relationship was normal—until R.S.S. cadres came to preach a new kind of intolerant Hinduism in three parts. Under the protective umbrella of the Central Government, the RSS cadres arrived to sow the seeds of discord and warned even Kerala, which had a tradition of amity between Hindus on one side and the Muslims and Christians, on the other.

In this connection, the tour of Gopal Godse, the brother of Mahatma Gandhi's assassin Nathuram Godse, in towns of Uttar Pradesh may be mentioned. Feeling proud of being co-accused in the assassination case, he declared at a meeting in Lucknow that the salvation of India lay in the philosophy in which Nathuram Godse believed. India should be a Hindu state, he added, like Pakistan which was a Muslim State.

It is certainly not coincidental that Gopal Godse's visit to each city and town was generally followed by Hindu-Muslim tension and riots. The holocaust in Aligarh was described by Harikishen Surjeet, the C.P.I. (M) leader thus: "wherever the atrocities had been committed against Muslim minority they were committed by the communalists". He held the Janata responsible for what happened in the city.

President, Krishna Kumar Nauman, the local R.S.S. leader, was responsible "for the holocaust in Aligarh".

This evidence of the prominent member of the Communist Party of India (Marxist) which was an informal ally of the Janata Party, was significant. Kalyan Singh, an R.S.S. Minister from the Janata Government in Uttar Pradesh was specially sent to Aligarh. He promptly used his Ministerial authority to get all the arrested leaders of R.S.S. released.

These were some of the talking points of Indira Gandhi with which she won the Chikmagalur seat in the Lok Sabha.

The Janata leadership was now revealing its true colours. Despite the election-time repprochement with Janata, the Communists (M) were up in arms against the "Black Bill". They brought two lakhs of workers from all parts of India to Delhi, and spoke in the voice of 81 year old S.S. Mirajkar, former Mayor of Bombay. He thundered, as he had never before, "This Parliament of the Working Class has rejected the Janata Government's Black Bill!"

This was being read by Indira Gandhi in one of the dailies. Now she could not say she had no time to read the reports on the socio-economic realities of India—her India—with which she could no longer afford to remain unconcerned.

7

Chikmagalur to Tihar Jail

"Jodi tor dak shune keu na asha, tobe ekla chalo re,
ekla chalo re"
(If nobody responds to your call, walk alone,
walk alone).
—RABINDRANATH TAGORE

"Main akela hi chala tha janib-e-manzil magar,
Loge saath sate gaye aur Carvaan banta gaya."
(I had started alone for the destination, but
the people kept on coming and thus the whole caravan
was formed).
—MAJROOH SULTANPURI

THE WHOLE town of Chikmagalur turned out to welcome Indira Gandhi.

She had chosen this out-of-the-way place for the bye-election because this was the only seat which was vacant. This would help her get into the Lok Sabha to carry on the fight from within the legislature and be able to speak out her mind on the fair and unfair remarks made about her 'crimes' and 'sins' almost every day.

The Janata Party people—specially Charan Singh, whose *bette noir* was Jawaharlal Nehru, abused and criticized for almost everything that was wrong in the country. Everything was bad because of Jawaharlal Nehru! As a daughter and disciple of Nehru, it became her duty to seek readmission to the Lok Sabha through a bye-election. And Chikmagalur was one of the small towns with several villages in Karnataka from where she could stand for the bye-election!

The mass of people whom she was seeing for the first time—mostly women—looked illiterate. So she could not establish a rapport with them either through English or Hindi. But she decided to address them in Hindi and see whether they could understand her or not.

She began her speech by addressing them as *"Bhaiyo aur Behano"* (brothers and sisters!); she was heartened to receive a thunderous applause on uttering these two words!

"Indira Gandhi", the crowd raised a slogan *"Zindabad"*.

'Indira Gandhi Zindabad!' How did they know this word which was *Persian*. It was one of the Urdu words, now a part of the vocabulary of Indian politics, made famous and popular by Sardar Bhagat Singh. He raised this slogan, after throwing a small bomb in the Central Assembly in Delhi and got world-wide publicity when he shouted defiantly: *"Inquilab Zindabad"*.

"Inquilab Zindabad", the words had entered the dictionary of Indian politics.

"Inquilab Zindabad"—the first word was Arabic and meant a Revolution, the gigantic social turning-over, which was understood and used by revolutionaries of all lands from Tashkent and Samarkand to Kabul and Tehran and now Delhi!

"Inquilab Zindabad", shouted Iranian oil-workers to sum-up their revolutionary demands.

"Inquilab Zindabad", was the chorus of the Afghan revolutionary students.

"Inquilab Zindabad", shouted Khan Abdul Ghaffar Khan's *Khudai Khidmatgars* (Servants of God) when they rose against the government of the British Resident.

"Inquilab Zindabad" was the cry of terrorist young revolutionaries as also of the non-violent volunteers as they paraded the streets of Lahore and Amritsar.

"Inquilab Zindabad", shouted in a strange chorus by Muslims and Hindus and Sikhs when the whole population came out in the streets to join a Congress procession.

"Inquilab Zindabad", shouted the Marathi-speaking workers

[53]

and Gujarati ladies when they defied the edict of the Governor in taking out a procession which was stopped at Bori Bunder.

"Inkeellab Jindabad"—mispronounced the Gujarati ladies and gentlemen when they paraded the main roads of Ahmedabad.

"Inkilaab Zindabad", shouted the Hindu and Muslim workers and peasants of Telangana in the Nizam's dominion.

"Inquilaab Jindabad", shouted the workers, peasants and students of Kerala as they imbibed a revolutionary ideology on the streets of Trivandrum and Cochin.

Indira Gandhi prefaced her remarks by mentioning to the audience the history of this Arabic-Persian phrase. It had become more popular in India than in the Persian speaking countries and in the original Arabic. That is India! A land of many languages, each developed and mature. Each language adopted words from other languages, such as English, French, and Portuguese; words like button, shirt, jacket, hat, books, railway, telegram, line, ticket, telephone; radio and television.

These words adopted from the European languages gave a common phraseology to our advanced languages: Hindi, Urdu, Gujarati, Marathi, Telugu, Malayalam and Kannada. Some of these languages were derived from Sanskrit which also gave a common phraseology. But with political workings of consciousness, political phrases like *Inquilab Zindabad* crept in.

Following the tradition of her revered father, she adopted simple language and conversational style of speaking, without the flourish of oration, making the contents of her speech understandable even to those whose knowledge of Hindi was patchy.

Thanks to the popularity of Hindi films, everybody in Chikmagalur knew the Bombay-Hindi and therefore could, more or less, understand the contents of her speech. They knew what she was saying, though they themselves were not well-versed in Hindi and could not articulate in the National language.

That evening, she realised, was an educational session for her, too. Now she knew that even aesthetically bad Hindi films did good to the people by familiarising them with the national language. Some of the people themselves had been to Bombay. A percentage of them were students in various schools, and they had read at least one or two Hindi text-books. So she was glad that even in the South (perhaps minus Tamil Nadu) Hindi had now become common currency of conversation!

Around Chikmagalur, there are green hills famous for their tea and coffee estates. The highest of them is the Baba Budan. A local legend tells us that a Muslim saint called Baba Budan came from holy Mecca, the centre of *Haj* for all the world's Muslims, bringing with him some coffee-seeds, which he threw on the ground. So thus coffee plantations grew up in this vicinity.

Once upon a time Chikmagalur was famous for its coffee trade and was a prosperous town. Now that distinction has gone, for coffee seeds which grew here are now grown in many places in South India. But Chikmagalur remains still famous for its coffee. Its people are relaxed and easy-going, and the Baba Budan tradition persists. There are many Muslims in Chikmagalur forming quite a prosperous community. They also voted enthusiastically for Indira Gandhi, for already she was known for being sympathetic towards the minorities. Chikmagalur has a tradition for electing a Congressman from this constituency. In 1971 it had elected Chandra Gowda who won this seat for the Congress. In 1978, when, he was elected to the Karnataka Legislative Council, he resigned from the Lok Sabha. The Karnataka Congress offered the seat to Indira Gandhi.

She had to contend with Virendra Patil, the former Chief Minister of Karnataka. He was a good administrator and one who had brought much prosperity to the area. But now it was a struggle between an all-India figure and a prominent provincial politician. Patil was the Janata candidate. Harijans were about 30 per cent in the constituency. The story of Belchi was enough for them to rally round Indira Gandhi. The Muslims were a small minority but they voted for Indira, daughter of Jawaharlal Nehru. The Janata sent their four big guns—Babu Jagjivan Ram, Bahuguna, Chandra Shekhar and George Fernandes who tried their best to rouse communal and caste issues because Patil was a Lingayat, and there were many Lingayats in Chikmagalur.

But it was the *charisma* of Indira Gandhi that won the seat for her. The plantation labourers who were voting against the *diktat* of their proprietors were a decisive factor.

Despite a blistering poster war carried on by Janata leadership, both national and local, despite the pitiable sight of daughter of Snehlata Reddy, the film actress and an unfortunate victim of the Emergency, parading a shirt on which was written in big letters, "SHE KILLED MY MOTHER", despite a series of posters some of which were vulgar and the anti-Indira dramas staged in the villages, Indira Gandhi, by her back-breaking campaign and braving of violent attacks—Indira Gandhi received a lathi blow on her back which she never spoke of nor showed to anyone, except to Nirmala Deshpande, who was accompanying her—won the seat by a big margin of over 77,000. Witnesses to this election battle were a hundred journalists, cameramen and television units not just from India but also from all over the world.

From her side, there was only one slogan in *Hindi* which became very popular, *"Ek sherni sau langoor, phir jitenge Chikmagalur"*. One lioness and a hundred baboons—we will win Chikmagalur! It was the slogan which swept the villages and towns in this area.

On 8th November, she returned to Delhi, triumphant on her victory. The poll results were announced. She had defeated her Janata opponent by more than 77,000 votes. She announced her victory as really a "victory of the people".

Yet four days later, on 12th November, Mrs. Gandhi flew to London by Air India. A number of British journalists, in addition to her supporters and opponents, were present at Heathrow Airport. A correspondent asked her "Are you trying to make a comeback?" She smiled as she replied, "But where had I gone?"

The press conference dissolved in laughter.

Later she faced the demonstrations *for* and *against* her. On the right of her car, people booed her for her alleged excesses of the Emergency, waved placards asking her to go back, while on the left people waved Indian tricolour flags. As her car passed through the tunnel, she left her opponents and her supporters, all British resident Indians, facing each other. The street demonstrations, both *for* and *against* her, continued pursuing her during the week she was in the United Kingdom.

The Claridges Hotel seemed to be occupied by her supporters and colleagues, including A.P. Sharma, Darbara Singh, C.M. Stephen and Sheila Kaul, all former Ministers of hers in the Congress Government who would be again her colleagues. Also in London, and awaiting her arrival, was her daughter-in-law, Sonia Rajiv Gandhi. They had all flown on their own to meet her at Claridges.

The security was very strict at Claridges. The arrangements made by Scotland Yard were almost 'fool-proof' and included a squadron of Police dogs. She was received by the British Premier, for Margaret Thatcher knew that now that she was successful in entering the Parliament, she was likely to be India's Prime Minister again and, therefore, politicians of both Parties came into contact with her. She had come for the London celebrations of her father's birthday, but she also attended a meeting of the Commonwealth Parliamentary Association. The British politicians were quite sure that they were dealing not only with the ex-Prime Minister but also the future Prime Minister of India. Mrs. Indira Gandhi was such an attraction that there was a £ 20 per head dinner for her. Those who could not get dinner tickets were prepared to spend £ 100 for just a seat at the dinner!

Students of Cambridge arrived in London in a double-decker bus, a meeting which was a reminder of her own student days at Somerville College at Oxford.

At all public meetings, both with British and Indians in London, she answered all questions fired at her regarding the Emergency in India about which such lurid tales were published in the British press. Her answers were frank and bold.

"Do you know," a Cambridge student asked her, "about the excesses of the Emergency?"

"No", she replied.

"If that is so," said the student, "does it not prove that you are both incompetent and incapable?"

"No," Mrs. Indira Gandhi said, "the Prime Minister did not, indeed, should not, interfere with state governments. Even the American President did not know what the C.I.A. did."

"But how can you disown responsibility?"

"Of course, that was why I took the responsibility on myself, though I did not know what was happening. India, as you know, is a big country."

Once or twice there were contradictions, too, in her statements.

About excesses in connection with family planning, she first said, "it had caught the imagination of the masses", and in the next breath, she said, "the poor were very much against it, because they have been brought up with the idea that children are God's gifts."

"But," she added, "this very idea has become a danger for India. There are 684 million in India, according to 1980 census. (Now there are more—K.A.A.). Every minute 40 children are born in India."

She concluded this argument with a reference to Abraham Lincoln, Lenin, Mao Tse Tung, Tito and Brezhnev, who stood up courageously, with conviction and dedication, for their beliefs which have prevailed against the test of time, and have brought changes for the benefit of mankind.*

Back in India, the very next day she had to be sworn in as the Honourable Member from Chikmagalur. She arrived at the main Gate A of Parliament House punctually at 10.50 a.m. There was a horde of photographers and newsreelers present to record the arrival of the ex-Prime Minister, who would be the next Prime Minister in a few months.

There was so big a crowd at Gate A, that she had to turn to a smaller gate, hoping that it would be free of the crowd. But the crowd behind her and inside the circular lobby made it difficult for her to make her entrance, and entered the House at one minute before eleven. The Congress members thumped their desks and shouted "Indira Gandhi Zindabad" while the Janata Party members cried "Shame, Shame"! She had already informed the Speaker that she had just arrived from London, and was coming to be sworn in.

She was used to the Seat Number One at the head of the Treasury Benches, but today she took a back seat along with two of her Congress colleagues—P.V. Narasimha Rao and C.M. Stephen.

There was again some heckling as she stood up and presented

*For much information in this chapter I am grateful to Darbari sisters' excellent book, INDIRA GANDHI'S 1028 DAYS (of being out of office), published by them from their residence at S-508, Greater Kailash, Part I, New Delhi. Price Rs. 40/-.

herself before the Speaker's table. Now she gave the Treasury Members another surprise. She took her oath in her halting Kanarese language which most of them could not understand. There were no cheers from the Janata Party members, occupying the Treasury Benches, but she treated everyone and specially the Speaker with due courtesy and decorum. Many were the insults that were hurled at her—but she only smiled in return.

There was yet another attempt to heckle her in court after the blunder of their last effort to imprison her in a court case.

There was an earlier attempt to incarcerate her in a Hrayana dak bungalow, the same in which some Janata leaders were detained, but by her versatility in knowing the legal loopholes and her lawyer appearing on the Haryana border, she was prevented from crossing over into Haryana. So they had to be more circumspect this time to put her behind bars.

Mrs. Indira Gandhi's popularity was again on the upward curve. Fence-sitters were already jumping into her party which called itself CONGRESS(I). So this time the Janata Government had to be extra-shrewd.

The action would be taken by the Parliamentary Committee of Privileges.

On the 7th of January, the Committee of Privileges took up the case. By January 17 the Committee was ready with its report. Mrs. Gandhi was ordered to appear before the Committee to give evidence in connection with the alleged "intimidation, harassment and institution of false cases against certain officials who were collecting information for answers to certain questions in the Lok Sabha on Maruti Limited."

It took a whole year to complete the report and it was discussed intermittently. After Mrs. Gandhi was sworn-in as a member, it was taken up for serious discussion in the Lok Sabha, on 13th December 1978.

She made a very effective speech in her own defence, excerpts from which are reproduced here:

.... I should like to submit with the utmost sincerity that I would cheerfully sacrifice even my life, let alone the membership of this House. If by so doing I could promote the cause of our country. As a British poet has written 'all else must be sacrificed to this cause, I fear no hardship, I have counted the cost'. The Janata Party knows and the Prime Minister knows, indeed, every man, woman and child in India know that if the drama of a kind of my impeachment, of a former Prime Minister is enacted, its sole purpose is not to solve any national problem but to silence a voice which they find inconvenient.

And, concluding her speech, she said:

I am a small person, but I have stood for certain values and objectives. Every insult hurled at me will rebound, every punishment inflicted on me will be a source of strength to me. My voice will not be hushed for it is not a lone voice. It speaks not for myself, a frail woman and unimportant person, it speaks not for a so-called 'total evolution' involving smugglers, dacoits and such others, but for the deep and significant changes in society which alone can be the basis of true democracy and a fuller freedom, which alone can ensure justice, and help to create a better man.

The atmosphere in this House has been reminiscent of the scene in Alice in Wonderland, when all the cards rise up in the air and shout, 'off with her head'. My head is yours. My box has been packed these several months, we had only to put in the winter things.

On 19th December came the decision to expel her from Parliament and the stipulation of how much time she must spend in jail.

This resolution was moved by the gallant Prime Minister Morarji Desai. No other business was done that day and Speaker K.S. Hegde adjourned the House 50 minutes before time. The Congress members who were incensed rushed to form a ring round her and started shouting slogans, "*Indira Gandhi Zindabad*" but when one of them started shouting "*Morarji Desai Murdabad*", she immediately stopped them from doing so.

When a woman M.P. approached her to give a message to other M.P.'s of her party, she intoned a verse, much, much popular in public schools:

> Wish me luck as you wave me good-bye,
> With a cheer,
> not a tear,
> In your eye.
> Give me a smile
> I can keep
> all the while
> that I am away.

Then she boarded her car from parliament straight to Tihar Jail. There she was surrounded by Congress M.P.'s and others from the public, who were all so incensed that there would have been a breach of peace, hadn't Indira Gandhi pleaded with them for non-violence.

Many people could not sleep that night, worrying about her. Was it the end of Indira Gandhi?

She was in the infamous Tihar Jail for seven days.

Part of the time she read books including Tagore's works; at other times she rested. She went to sleep early but did not give up waking at her usual hour.

At 7.30 p.m., as she came out of jail, it was calculated that she had spent only 105 hours and 25 minutes in prison.

There was a small crowd at the jail gates, because the time of her release was not published, but there was a big crowd at her house—including the press men.

She did not look a tragic figure; she seemed to have enjoyed the compulsory rest in Tihar Central Jail. She was in high spirits as she stood on a chair to address the Press and the people.

From that day the count-down of the Janata Party rule had begun.

8

Resurrection

"Election, Membary, Council, Sadarat, Banaye khoob Azadi ne phande."
(Elections, Membership, Council, Presidentship, Freedom has done well to make her snares).

—IQBAL

THE JANATA Party was obsessed with Indira Gandhi.

It, like any class of *nouveau riche* did not know what to do with her.

Suffering as its members were from an inferiority complex, they were all out to humiliate her, and to the maximum extent.

But, as we know, no one can be humiliated unless he or she is willing to be humiliated.

True, she was the author of the dictatorial Emergency.

True, she and/or her colleagues, her second son, and officials, were responsible for many 'excesses' of the Emergency.

True, her Information Minister and the Censorship did curb and control the independence and self-expression of the Press and the Media.

True, her Emergency Regime was guilty of arresting and jailing many of those who constituted the Janata Party and the Janata Government in those days.

But let us not forget that she also, by a stroke of her 'dictatorial' pen, removed the shackles of the Emergency and ordered the Parliamentary Election of March 1977—which set into motion the forces which brought into being the Janata Party and the Janata Government.

She was not only the doting mother of Sanjay Gandhi, she also 'mothered' the Janata Party and the Janata victory!

Whichever way, whether she did or not, does it mean that the Janata Party should 'bore' us to death with the one problem of Indira Gandhi? Her Emergency or pre-Emergency 'excesses' to the exclusion of the much more important problems of the country—like poverty, unemployment, housing, education, law and order—which called for Governmental attention, for solution and resolution?

During the Janata regime hardly a day passed when, in one form or the other, Indira Gandhi came into the political spotlight whether the spotlight was correctly focussed on her or not for better or worse.

It started with all sorts of rumours and maligning gossip—immediately after the end of the Emergency! A plane was standing ready at the Delhi airport to take her, her family and her 'ill-gotten' riches (tons of baggages was mentioned!) to a foreign destination. The name of Italy, the home of her daughter-in-law, was specifically mentioned, with alleged 'Mafia' connections! Exaggeration of her faults and menace served in her interest and discredited her enemies and victims.

Actually she made no move to go anywhere—she decided to stay put in India and in New Delhi, though in a new and smaller house. There, she converted a little corner room for her office with but a single typewriter; and there she conducted the press and television interviews with national and international media.

It was here that I met and interviewed her for my book, *20th March 77—A DAY LIKE ANY OTHER DAY!* when I found her subdued, contrite, and even repentant about some of the 'excesses'. But the barrage of attacks upon her, describing her as an unmitigated fascist dictator, had the reverse effect on her. She stopped being apologetic about the 'excesses' of the Emergency, she said she had done no wrong and would stand by her son, Sanjay, and all that he did or got done by others. The over-kill of all the exaggerated charges against her led her to a more resolute —and even arrogant —stance.

Then came the farce of her 'arrest' and release immediately after. Just when the (then) Home Minister was holding a press conference explaining why she had been arrested, she was freed on bail and was holding a press conference on her own. The same evening she flew to Bombay from where, after a night's rest, she proceeded by road to Gujarat—getting there a tumultous reception from peasants (and specially women) in Morarji Desai's home state.

Later on, she applied for a passport to go to England where she had been invited to participate in the celebrations of her father's birth anniversary. There were objections to it, as well as allegations and innuendos, that she might not return to face the charges of the Shah Commission and the Court. She was given a restricted passport.

A representative of the U.K. Government and Deputy High Commissioner for India were among those who received her. She proved thereby that she did not have to be Prime Minister (or a dictator) to be cordially received in another country. She defended herself in her speeches which, indeed, won her some sympathy and even admiration. She returned via Moscow where, during one hour's stop-over, she was met by one high official of the Soviet Government.

By returning within the stipulated period, she confounded her detractors who had suspected her of trying to get out and away from India. She certainly improved her international image after the London visit.

Now she had been sentenced to a 7-day prison term and expelled from Parliament for an offence which was committed (if at all) years ago when another Parliament was in session.

The Allahabad decision of the High Court held her responsible for two Electoral 'Crimes'—one was that she addressed an election meeting from a dais (prepared not by her but *for* her certainly) made by the U.P. (Congress), which was higher than, the height permissible under Electoral Rules. Her other 'crime' was to appoint as her Electoral Agent a man whose resignation from Government service had not been accepted twenty-four hours earlier than stipulated. These were technical and small lapses for which she was jailed, and not 'crimes' that were exaggerated and boosted, as if they were *moral* crimes committed by her. If the idea behind the short prison term was to humiliate her, it was likely to boomerang on those who had sentenced her. For they, of all the people, should know that Indians love and respect political leaders who have the guts to suffer a prison term. After all, most of them won the last elections simply because Indira Gandhi had committed the mistake to lock them up during the Emergency. That was what gave even RSS and the communalist Muslims political respectability. Haven't the Janata Party leaders, by arresting her, committed the same mistake in reverse?

Certainly Indira Gandhi faced her Parliamentary punishment with cheerful courage and conviction. Whatever else she may be, she certainly knew how to play the political game, with some dignity and decorum, which is more than can be said of her political adversaries!

* * *

The world thinks that only ONE skylab plummetted in the Indian Ocean.

But Indians know better. One was the skylab that was sent up by NASA in the U.S.A. It went up into space, then circled the earth thousands of times, sending television pictures of the earth and other data. It functioned very well, but since solar energy was its only source of power, it continued to fall in space, by one kilometre every year.

So after six years, as it was calculated later, it re-entered the earth's atmosphere, which caused friction and burning, turning it into a ball of fire. Its functioning, which had kept it afloat in space came to a standstill. It plummetted to the earth and drowned in the depths of the Indian Ocean.

The other skylab which plummetted to the earth at Delhi— a place where great empires have come toppling down—was known as the JANATA GOVERNMENT. Like the American skylab this was also a beetle-shaped creature with several wings.

The main body of this one, known as the Cong-O, was hollow inside. It had four wings known as the Bharatiya Lok Dal, the

Jan Sangh, the Congress For Democracy, and the Socialists. When it went up, there rose a great and hopeful jubilation in the land. But it soon started malfunctioning from the very start. Its wings were unequal and oddly-shaped and this upset its centrifugal force.

It, however, kept afloat for some time even though there was no conventional fuel or a cementing element involved. This was largely due to the spinning top-principle which keeps it going round and by which even hollow things keep afloat in space for a time. But then the power of each wing asserts itself and the centre, being hollow and puny, it cannot keep the unnatural contraption together.

So after a year this skylab began to rattle and squeak and creak. Cracks appeared in its polished surface and the saffron paint began to peel off. Underneath the paint of Opportunism was revealed the tin which is the basest of all base metals.

Raj Narain, along with a substantial chunk of fifteen Janata M.P.s, was the first to part company from the strange contraption. Having once lost balance, the other parts tended to break away. By the afternoon of July 11, as many as 46 vital parts of this Indian skylab dropped down into the ocean of Indian politics, where they were swallowed-up by the crocodiles of other Parties. Meanwhile, the Urine-powered hollow robot pilot kept on reassuring his various components that all was well with the ship of State—or the skylab!

Indira Gandhi certainly played a political 'game' with her opponents and the detractors of her father and family, by playing one against the other. When their strength in Parliament was so balanced she with her 77, could play a decisive role in the political game of Charan Singh as against Morarji Desai.

She did not have to reveal her intentions—she only took advantage of political conditions and the conflicting ambitions of the Janata leaders.

First, she supported Charan Singh through her Party of less

than hundred M.P.'s against Morarji Desai. And then, she allowed them to vote against Charan Singh to bring him down only after a few days of his term.

Surely it was not what Jawaharlal Nehru would have done. But then he was a gentleman. And Jawaharlal had not been overwhelmed with this kind of opposition which his daughter had to deal with.

A day later, when the Vote of No-Confidence was moved by the Opposition and passed came the end. Or was it?

The lesson is that, with four wings sprouting from the main cylindrical stump, you can keep a spinning top revolving for some time, but not for all times.

Or, to vary the metaphor, as the old, old adage has it, you can fool some people for some time, but not all the people all the time.

*   *   *

Jayaprakash Narayan, the Gentleman-Architect who had been responsible for the Janata victory and the defeat of Indira Gandhi, died in October 1979, after a long and tortuous illness.

J.P. died a completely disillusioned man. The *sampurna kranti* (total revolution) of which he had dreamed and for which he had worked, was never realized.

The infrastructure of self-sufficient Gandhian village republics remained as his distant ideal.

On the other hand, he saw, with his failing health, the rampant corruption, nepotism, in-fighting in the Janata ranks, which could not have been a source of revived will-power, the will to live.

J.P. was now a hallowed hero—even a martyr in the Janata cause, but, while he lived, he had already become expendable... he was a mere figurehead, seldom consulted by those whom he had himself placed in the seats of power and authority.

J.P.—idealist, freedom-fighter, revolutionary, anti-authoritarian, anti-Communist, Gandhi-ite, critic of Nehru and houseguest of Seth Ramnath Goenka—was a paradox and a bundle of contradictions, like all great men. He was an enigma. Few could come up to his expectations, few (not even he himself) could practise his ideals. That was his tragedy—and also his glory.

* * *

It was not the *Return* of the Red Rose. It was Return *to* the Red Rose—so it was hoped.

It was not a renewal of the hereditary claims of Indira Gandhi. She discarded the symbol of her father's *Red* Rose when she, under the Emergency, tried to impose a personal or family dictatorship. She discarded the *Red* Rose and was, in her turn, discarded by the votaries of the *Red* Rose though, in their simpleminded ignorance, they opted for a thorny cactus.

I mean return to the ideology of Nehru, as symbolized by the Red Rose.

* * *

Kuldip Nayar of the *Indian Express*, I was glad to note, had at last come to proclaim in favour of the "consensus he (Nehru) had built behind certain fundamentals like parliamentary democracy, secularism, socialism, non-alignment and modernisation". What Nehru would have liked to call the development of the "Scientific Temper" (among the superstition-ridden people of India !)

Thus, after two years of amendment of Nehruism by his own daughter and grandson, and two years of the wilful distorted presentation of Nehruism by his old foes and political adversaries like Chaudhari Charan Singh, once again there was a renewal of interest in Nehru and Nehruism, in his vision of a socialist, secular and democratic India, in his advocacy of the Scientific Approach to problems of the country and the world.

I saw Kuldip Nayar's article in that context. Even his critics and detractors are now seeing the wisdom of the Nehru ideology. It began with Atal Behari Vajpayee (the least irrational of the Jana Sangh clan!) finding himself in the room of Jawaharlal Nehru, and in his shoes as Foreign Minister and, after criticising him for a decade, realizing that Nehru's ideology of non-alignment and Nehru's partiality for the socialist world was the most practical and perfect policy for India, in response to the imperatives of History. So far as Socialism and Secularism are concerned, they are built-in features of the Indian ethos. No one can make a headway with the Indian people (that is what the failure and ultimate disappearance of the Swatantra Party taught the others!) without, at least, paying lip-service to these two tenets of Nehruism.

That is what Nehru had achieved in his lifetime—the ·people were converted to Socialism through his three decades of "wandering among Kisans" and talking to them when he was just a Congress leader and, later, when he was Prime Minister. He compromised with many personalities (some of them known to be corrupt and crooked, even opposed to him and his ideology); but he never compromised on principles. He always hoped in the end the Principle will triumph, the personality will improve or change for the better, would be changed by social forces to remould itself. This was, in another way, Gandhiji's hope also.

Kuldip Nayar said that once Nehru was asked why practically every Party talked in terms of Socialism, his reply (so said Kuldip Nayar) was that it went down well with the masses.

Nehru never (or hardly ever) spoke of the people as "masses". What he probably would have said was that the people, because they are poor, instinctively want Socialism (or the essence of Socialism), and that is why, in a poor country, every Party is compelled to speak in terms of Socialism.

The same is true of Secularism—despite the occasional aberrations of communal riots. Peace (it has been said) is built in Man's genes. Man is the only animal who does not eat his own species. The cannibals are exceptions.

Religious toleration is likewise built-in in the Indian Ethos. It comes naturally—that is why Parties must speak of Secularism also. Even religious parties (like the Muslim League and the Hindu Mahasabha, whatever their aims) must speak of Secularism and religious tolerance—otherwise they cannot hope to attract any votes.

*   *   *

[69]

Twenty-eight days remained, out of Mrs. Indira Gandhi's 1028 days of *Ban Vas* to be over.

The same with what Nayar calls "Modernisation". What Nehru would have called the "Scientific Approach" or the "Scientific Method". He wanted Indians to adopt an empirical attitude, not a dogmatic, religious attitude, on the socio-economic problems. This satisfies the Indian people's basic urge and aspirations to be modern, scientifically equipped to face competition in a modern, scientific world. Some (like intellectuals) do it consciously, others (like simple-minded common people) do it sub-consciously.

The Nehru Ethos (or the *Indian* Ethos)—Socialism, Secularism and World Peace—thus responded to the needs and aspirations of the Indian people. That is why when Nehru explained these components to the people, they listened to him. It was like someone telling them their own inner-most thoughts. That was the secret of his popularity and the basis of his leadership.

His views were opposed always by reactionaries and obscurantists, never by the people even though some people were misled by reactionaries and obscurantists. There was a consensus on Nehru's Ideology, for it represented what was GOOD for the People of India.

It was GOOD for the People.

It *is* still Good for the People.

The people can still be rallied round the banner of Nehruism.

If only the true Nehruites—not hereditary Nehruites but *ideological* Nehruites—can present a Nehruvian alternative to the people in India.

*   *   *

There was a time when it used to be said that "There is only one MAN in the Central Cabinet—bold enough to take important decisions—and 'his' name was Indira Gandhi!"

Then came the Sanjay half-decade when it was felt that Indira was getting 'old' and that due to her weakness as an Indian mother the power was slipping into the hands of her younger son.

Since Sanjay's untimely and unfortunate death, once again it could be said that there was only one MAN in the Central Cabinet—'he' was characteristically youthful and dynamic—and 'his' name was Indira Gandhi!

Not only had she shown "poise and dignity" after Sanjay's death (as Inder Malhotra rightly noted in his article "Back To Work In Delhi" in the *Times of India*). "Indeed she has set the pace which is faster than the one prevailing in official Delhi".

At the same time it was felt that henceforward there would be no *subjective* initiative and actions which took away some of Sanjay's dynamism and, probably, caused his untimely death.

Objectivity and Maturity were back in the chair of authority—as also her old concern for the weaker sections of Society.

Her talk to the Yough Congress (I) workers was a pointer in the *right* (or, rather, LEFT) direction. Addressing an extended meeting of the Youth Congress National Executive, she directed them to go to the masses and educate them (her father would have said to "learn" *from* the masses) and "ensure that politically-motivated issues did not get over-riding prominence over human tragedy."

To illustrate her point, she mentioned the Baghpat incident and described it as 'reprehensible' (while, according to a pamphlet issued by the local Youth Congress workers, which echoes the Police view-point entirely dismisses the whole incident as Police action against drunken dacoits). So her characterising it as 'reprehensible' was an oblique reprimand to the Youth Congress workers.

She wanted Youth Congress workers to restore a balance and to present events to the public in "proper perspective" so as not to inflame them but rather to educate them.

But the most important (and the most Nehruvian) part of her speech was when she analysed the situation. "Unlike many countries in the West, India had gone through a political revolution first and now awaited an *economic revolution*. Youth power" she said, "could be harnessed for the benefit of the masses."

The "five *new* points" added to the Sanjay Gandhi five point programme bore the original Nehruvian stamp of Indira Gandhi. These were (1) Protection of, and service to, the socially disadvantaged, (2) creating avenues of self-employment for rural urban youth, through vocational training, (3) fight against anti-social practices like dowry, (4) help prevent waste of food and energy and vulgar display of wealth in social ceremonies, and (5) to help to improve life in the villages.

The Prime Minister should have cautioned the votaries of Youth Power not to do all this in an arrogant, and authoritarian manner—then it would not be 'service' of the poor, and would be authoritarian dictatorship instead of 'education'.

The programme of action set down before Youth was correct, the emphasis on 'education' and 'service' of the disadvantaged masses was correct and dynamic. This was truly a Youthful programme. But from the heights of Age and Responsibility, the Prime Minister ought to have added a cautionary warning to the Youth not to become rubber-stamps of Authority.

On 14th January 1980, Mrs. Indira Gandhi mounted the stairs of the Council Chamber and walked directly into seat 1 in the Treasury benches. The 1028 days of her *Banwas* was over, and now she was not afraid of anything. She was being sworn in as Prime Minister for the fourth time in her life.

9

※

Return to South Block

"All this will not be finished .... Nor will it be finished
in the present five thousand days, nor in the life of this
administration, nor perhaps, in their life-time on this
planet. *But let us begin*!"

—John F. Kennedy

The return to South Block was uneventful.

Indira, when she entered the Prime Minister's office, felt as if
she had been away for a prolonged holiday—1028 days. She took
to her work in the same manner. Nothing was changed—even
the portrait of Nehru had been replaced on the wall in its original position.

The swearing-in ceremony was at the Rashtrapati Bhavan. The
President was courtesy itself, though he had himself only a few
months earlier, called upon Charan Singh to take the same oath.
There was a formidable barrage of microphones before her and a
modest turn-out of movie cameras. The same night it would be
no the screens of India and the capitals of the world.

There had been a Lok Sabha election in January 1980. She
had contested from two constituencies. This time she had chosen
Medak in Andhra Pradesh and Rae Bareli in Uttar Pradesh, and
won both the seats. She won both the seats resoundingly. The
Janata Party had put Rajmata Vijayaraje Scindia (the Mother
of the young Congressman, the Madhavrao Scindia of Gwalior!).
Indira won against the Janata Rani by 1,23,654 votes, while the
Medak seat was won by 2,13,134 votes. So she resigned from

[73]

Rae Bareli seat and retained the Medak constituency. She wanted to repay this new connection till the end. For, after all, the South had been consistently loyal to her through thick and thin. She being the Hon'ble Member from Medak would be a shining example of National Integration, and would remain so for ever.

When alone, she reminisced about her re-entry into office. Doubtless she had played a political game—made Morarji Desai fight it out with Charan Singh—and wondered whether her father, were he alive, would have approved of his daughter playing this game? He was a victim of his own *sharafat*, his gentleman-liness. If he had held the referendum in Kashmir in 1950-51 when Kashmiris were in revolt against Pakistan, India would have won very easily. But again his *sharafat* came in the way. He had said no plebiscite or referendum was possible unless normalcy prevailed in Kashmir. So Pakistan saw to it that normalcy would not return. It was to their advantage to keep the pot boiling by sending tribal raiders every now and then! But India had missed the opportunity. The 'Emergency'—at least some aspects of it—served an ill-wind. Today she was to reap the whirl-wind!

Once safely and securely ensconced in her Prime Ministerial chair, she had to examine all the problems of the country—scientific problems, the motor cars (which was Sanjay's problem), foodstuff prices, customs and tarrif, inflow of foreigners, the percentage of tourists, oil (for energy and power) crisis, the rising prices and lowering life-spans! That brought to her mind the problem of her Sanjay's 'Maruti', about which there was a scandal. There were some hecklers who were never tired of asking questions in Parliament. And from tomorrow she would be in Parliament to answer their questions. How was she to cope with all these questions?

She must tell Sanjay to lie low for some time—no use giving interviews to comely editors. They got you nowhere except in trouble! The difficulty was that he had no alibi which could escape attention. Let the Maruti problem rest for a while.

She was still re-adjusting her strategies, when her Press Secretary entered with a sheaf of Press Cuttings.

"What is this?" she queried. "The Press—you know I don't read it."

"But, madam this is important."

"What is it?" she asked.

Sorting out the clippings, he laid them down for her perusal. One was with a double-column heading, "BIHAR BLIND-INGS—Harijans in jail tortured". The other was a single-column box item from another paper. "HARIJANS BLINDED—Jail horrors from Bihar."

She reluctantly read this item. Date-lined Bhagalpur (Bihar), it told a gruesome tale of dacoity, the Harijans were overpowered by the policemen and acid was poured into their eyes which were gouged out with a pen-knife.

This was horrible enough. But, what was worse still is that there were photographs of the blind people. She closed her eyes. But, after a while, she opened them. Even a few minutes of 'Self-blindness' was horrible. Suppose she had been one of them! Suppose when she opened her eyes, she could not see! It would be horrible, excruciatingly horrible. She put the clippings back into the folder which the Press Secretary had considerately left behind on her desk.

She looked at her watch. It was a few minutes to one o'clock, She looked at the calendar of appointments. It was blank. Perhaps her Secretaries were not expecting her to come to the office that day itself. But once sworn-in, she had to attend office. She must make it clear to them at once. Now soon it will be lunch time.

She got up from her chair and shouted for her bearer. She rang the bell. The bearer came in at once.

"*Hum khana khane ja rahe hain. Aur kal se kaam shuru karen-gay. Sab logon se kahdo.*" We are going to have our lunch. From tomorrow we shall be here both times. *Tell everyone.* Then she went to the door.

The driver was asleep at the steering wheel of the car. "*Ghar chalo,*" she briefly ordered him, and the tone she used was re-primand enough.

On the way she opened the newspaper. From the front-page a headline hit her eyes. "ONE MORE DOWRY DEATH—The Unfortunate Bride Has Left a Letter Accusing the P.M. For Not Caring For the Plight of Her Sisters". That was reprimand

[75]

enough for her. But what could she do in the matter? God alone could bring about the change in the husband's heart and the mother-in-law's heart. But at least she, as a woman, could speak out, warning the would-be bridegrooms to desist from marriage if they or their parents expected too much from dowry! Had she ever done it? No, said her conscience and then more accusingly, "Why not?"

*   *   *

When her car came to a halt in the portico, she emerged from it. "*Daadi* is back!" rang out little Rahul's voice.

Rajiv's children were at school. Drawn by the voice of her son, Maneka also came out of her room. She namaskared her mother-in-law. Blessing her with "*Jiti raho*", she enquired about Sanjay. "He is back from the factory but you know what he looks like when he comes. So he is taking a bath. You will see him at the lunch table."

Indira was the first to arrive at the dining table, then came Sonia and Rajiv.

"What plane are you piloting, Rajiv?" The anxious mother asked.

"Still *Avros*. But next month I will be promoted to Boeings. Then I will be qualified enough to pilot the plane whenever you have to go abroad."

"Yes, I am sure of that."

Meanwhile, Sanjay, in plain white khaddar pyjama and kurta arrived with water dripping from his hair followed by Maneka.

"Maneka, you don't look after your husband properly. Look at his hair—dripping water which will soon drip into the soup."

Maneka took a towel from the towel-stand, and rubbed it into her husband's scalp.

"May be you will take more care", told the mother to her second son. "Look at Rajiv. Sonia does not allow him to come to the dining room with his hair dripping bath-water."

"Sanjay, what about those cans of that film made by some one in Bombay called—what's the name?

"*Kissa Kursi Ka*," answered Maneka.

[76]

"It has been crushed out of existence. I have an efficient crusher at the factory."

"What chair do they mean?"

"We have both seen it . . . Rajiv and Sonia refused to see it."

"Yes, I haven't time to see the trash they make in Bombay *philum* factories."

"You must train yourself not to make such sweeping remarks. Tell me, Sanjay, what was it like?"

"The usual Bombay stuff, *Maa*. But Shabana was good, I must say."

"You *will* say that!" Maneka was jealousy incarnate as she said it.

"Yes, I will say it—If I feel like it."

"Children—children!" warned Mrs. Indira Gandhi, "behave yourselves."

They all fell silent, and thereafter paid attention to little else, except the lunch plates before them.

By the time the lunch was over, and even the fruit dishes were removed, Sanjay had the floor. "*Maa*, tell me how did you feel the getting back to your office?"

"It was like any other day. But the staff needs time to adapt itself to my way of working!"

"You can't blame the poor blokes—they have been with people like Morarji and that fellow, Vajpayi!"

"Vajpayi proved the best of the whole Janata people," said Indira Gandhi. "He didn't change the foreign policy. He followed the example of Nehru-Indira policy in foreign affairs."

She smiled, while ruminating over most of her Minister colleagues having succumbed to the poor voter.

She wondered where, and how, were they—Bansilal, the *Chamcha* of Sanjay, the Defence Minister who had not been able even to defend himself. Where was Vidya Charan Shukla, the Information and Broadcasting Minister, appointed on Sanjay's recommendation. There was no *information* about him! There were many familiar faces not present in the new Lok Sabha. But, nevertheless, she had 370 members in the Lok Sabha, with new names.

Will she be able to make a cabinet of the new-comers? There were many younger and more enthusiastic members—called

[77]

Sanjay's men — but hardly the stuff of which the Ministers were made of! She had to pick and choose from 370 members. That was not the two-thirds majority that she wanted. That is what she needed to re-frame the Laws.

She thought all these things, and was overwhelmed by them. What about Harijans? One *Belchi* was not enough. That was not the end of it. True, she had created a sensation in the country. But, meanwhile, there had been many more of such incidents, and she could not visit all the places. There were bride-burnings in Delhi, some of them even in her new Delhi; and she had not visited one such place to console the *burnt* bride's parents. Her fourth term would have more economic, political, social and sociological problems. How did her father manage them and still keep his humour intact? That was true *charisma*! And they talked as if she had also a charisma of her own. Flatterers, appropriately called *Chamchas*! Oh God!

But at one time in the beginning of her first term she had confessed that she did not believe in God, though she believed in some supreme power, but certainly not in any rituals or *namaaz* and *roza*, or the grappings of *pujas* and such like . . . what did they call them? . . . Yes, *Havans* and *Mahayagnas*! But she had sacked one of her dynamic and young Ministers as she was told that he had a *havan* performed against her? She did not believe in them. Then why did she have him removed?

May be the report was false, may be it was exaggerated. The truth that once you are in a seat of power and authority, you couldn't pick and choose these spiritual gimmicks. You never were sure what was false and what was true? Even her father, during his last illness, used to take the *prasaad* from a temple— but had strictly *warned* the maid-servant to use the side entrance. After all, he had his rationalist reputation to protect!

What was Security? Till yesterday, she was quite *safe* in 12, Willingdon Crescent, but today, she was not safe in 1, Akbar Road. That also went with authority and power. She did not know how many policemen were required to guard her. What was it? Security or guarding the prisoner? She felt more and more like a prisoner of Power.

Thinking these thoughts a strange thing happened. She fell

asleep something which normally she never did. Her staff was aghast. She was sleeping in her drawing-room, while outside there were dozens of men—including V.I.P.'s—waiting for her *darshan*! Could they bring them in? No, that will never do. She was not only sleeping—she was also dreaming! She was having a frightful nightmare. She was blabbering in her sleep: No, *no*. No! As if she was surrounded by a gang of men, all armed with swords, pistols and sten-guns. She was soon awake! Her guards heaved a sigh of relief.

"Madam, I dare not awaken you! But the people are waiting for you in the ante room."

"What time is it?", she asked him. She could not look at her own watch!

"It's nearly four o'clock, Madam."

"Good Lord!" She exclaimed, "I finished lunch at about 2 o'clock. But I had a frightening dream with black-hooded people coming in to murder me. One had a revolver and the other had a sten-gun. Call the people one by one. But say nothing about my dream."

10

✿

The World's Largest Kitchen

"You can have everything in the world, but without morale it is largely ineffective. Morale is a state of the mind. It is steadfastness, courage and hope. It is confidence, zeal and loyalty. It is elan, *esprit de corps* and determination."

—GEORGE MARSHALL

WAS IT the wise *Kautilya* who said—or is it in one of the *Upanishads*?—that she had read that "A man is what he eats"?

That summed up the significance of Food-stuff in a national economy. So they had begged for PL-480 Wheat Aid from America—after all even the mighty Soviet Union had signed a treaty with the greatest capitalist nation when there was drought in the Eastern territories. There was nothing remarkable about accepting AID from America. Also in her heart of hearts, she knew that there was nothing shameful in taking this aid within this kind of the international community. You take the 'aid' even though, contrary to popular apprehensions, it is not *infra dig* for a nation to take the grain aid.

America was dependent on foreign 'aid'—which was a kind of *loan* that the producer gave with pleasure because it solved the problem of over-production.

You could not depend on it *forever*. Hence the 'Green Revolution' in Punjab. Here, by the use of (imported grain) fertilizers and modern methods of farming, like tractors (largely imported from U.S.S.R.) and other such mechanical devices for quick

[80]

disposal of the wheat harvest such as mechanized harvesters and large threshers and Combines, the yield was doubled—increasing the per capita income of the average farmer—though he largely depended on imported (from Bihar, Uttar Pradesh, and Rajasthan) labour which worked on daily basis.

Nehru knew that India would soon be confronted with the *kulak* class, but there was no escaping it. Into the rich soil of Punjab he supplied every agricultural input—the best of seeds, water from pumps, electricity reaching every village to man and mend the agricultural devices which were the product of Bhilai and other industrial plants, which he (with the friendly assistance from the Soviet Union) had set up though the oppositionists, like Chaudhary Charan Singh, were always running down as 'Nehruvian expansive gimmicks', even 'luxuries' that India could not afford.

But Nehru knew. He had not been raised in a farming family —yet he had done considerable 'walking' in the villages of U.P. as a young man who was most of the time using his legs from one village to another. He called it in his *Autobiography*: "WANDERING AMONG KISANS". He was full of compassion for them.

"Why don't they revolt?, he once asked. And Indira, then a teen-aged girl, instantly answered her father by saying, "They are waiting for a leader for decades! Will you be 'their leader'?" That non-plussed him, and he took refuge in the Congress work that was already too much for him. But she must do something for them. One Government which had lasted less than two years, had failed to improve matters. Now she must do something for them. But what?

As 1980 proceeded further, she was to receive the deadliest blow to her personally. Her second son, Sanjay, the apple of her eye, now no longer interested in his 'Maruti' project which had virtually closed, took to dare-devil flying. So he took off one morning and with an Air Force pilot went up and performed aerobatics over the house of his mother and the diplomatic colony. Once when his plane, while dipping dangerously, came low, his mother hearing the roar of the plane, went out in the verandah and called out "Who is that? She was informed that the plan was Sanjay's and that he was performing those flying tricks.

"There should be a law against performing such tricks, flying so low over populated areas!", she said. She was told by some of her aides that there *was* such a law but there was no one to restrain Sanjayji. In fact, now she remembered, the Director of Civil Aviation, Jaffer Zaheer, had drawn her attention to Sanjay's frequent flying antics. Indeed, so far she was aware Jaffer Zaheer had resigned on this very issue. Just then there was the sound of a crash, and something told her that it was Sanjay's plane. She ran wildly, got into her white Ambassador, and told the driver to go straight to the scene of the crash. "May be it is someone else," her common-sense told her, but the Mother in her would not be consoled. She reached the spot of the disaster, and even before she recognized him, her heart-beats told her that it would not be a sight for her to see. She disciplined her heart and looked at the bloody sight. Before some doctor arrived from the same vicinity, she knew that both the occupants of the plane were dead. Death must have been instantaneous.

She took off his watch and keys which were on the body, and later handed them over to Maneka who followed her in another car. "*Main ne in se kaha tha ke aaj aaraam karen, magar woh kab kisi ki baath suntay they!*" And she burst in a torrent of tears.

Sikhs and Hindus both were present at Sanjay's funeral. This was the last such occasion in the capital! Now she retired into herself while all the cremation ceremonies were duly performed. Maneka borrowed some courage from her mother-in-law's silent fortitude while mourning for her husband. She got her magazine rewritten to accommodate a flattering story on Sanjay written by her and (one presumes) corrected by Sardar Khushwant Singh. It was a brilliant, though by no means a comprehensive article by which the young widow was publicly acknowledging what she and the country had missed. She lost a great husband, and the nation, a great promising leader, who, but for this accident, would have been the next Prime Minister with her as the Prime Minister's spouse and the First Lady of this country.

For a week she observed the mourning period according to the Sikh tradition. Her mother-in-law was very sweet to her; Varun and Maneka was shown every possible consideration. The Prime Minister would take little Varun to her room and fondled him behind closed doors, sometimes shedding silent tears. But even she could not find an answer for the child's questions about his missing father, though he lisped the required syllables about his going above to God Almighty. He was reassured both by his mother and his *Daadi* that wherever he was, he was very happy.

Slowly the silent tears had been shed and Mrs. Indira Gandhi became her normal self. The nation—the people—came first. Occasionally she went out (and took Varun with her) to her farm in Mehrauli near the *Qutub Minar*, where he would enquire who made this lofty Minar? Has my father, the child wondered, gone up to meet God by climbing this tower?

Mrs. Gandhi had purchased and developed this farm for practical reasons. She had not liked the remark that Chester Bowles, the American Ambassador had made about her, that "she lacked the understanding of the process of economic development". Another leader of an Opposition Party had said that "she would not be able to distinguish between a paddy-field and a field of wheat." The trouble was both of them were right, but she wanted a farm of her own and there grow both paddy and wheat, and learn to distinguish between the two types of grains.

As a matter of fact, it was Nehru's policy of encouraging modern type of agriculture that had shown bright results. She had only kept it up. Thus the agricultural production had, after 1968, risen from year to year. And Food production had followed the pattern set by Nehru. It showed an upward trend for some years, dipping now and then, and finally reaching the original level.

What else was there in the national larder? Power generation which was in 1965-66, 33 billion units, rose up to 130 billion units. Oil which was only 3 million tons rose up to 21.1 million tons, coal which was 70.3 in 1965-66 rose upto 137.1 in 1982-83; likewise finshed steel which was 4.51 million tons rose upto 8.05 million tons in 1982-83; similarly fertilizer which was 344 thousand tons rose upto 440.40 thousand tons; paper which was 558 thousand tons in 1955-56 rose upto 1203 thousand tons; so also cement which was 10.8 thousand tons rose upto 23.2 thousand tons; commercial vehicles which were 35 thousand in 1965-66 rose upto 86,000 in 1982-83; production of cars and jeeps which were 35.4 thousand in 1965-66 rose by 1982 upto 65.4 thousand; cycles which were 1574 thousands rose upto 4890 thousands; electric fans which were 1753 thousands rose upto 4100 thousands; sugar which was 3610 thousand tons rose upto 8232; tea from 376 million kilograms rose upto 563 million kilograms; vanaspati rose from 401 thousand tons upto 886 thousand tons.

The economy in Mrs. Gandhi's regime continued the progress as it did under Jawaharlal Nehru (in the years 1965-66) which was 70 percent and rose upto 740 million rupees—that is it kept up the progress upto 150 percent thereby roughly keeping pace with the increased population. This was the danger of which Mrs. Indira Gandhi was mortally afraid. That is why she fell for the game of her second son. The poor breed too much and then they live in dirty slums. They create all kinds of problems for the decent folks. That was the litany Sanjay intoned before his mother!

No doubt, increased population was the root of many evils. There were no foodgrains to be fairly and equitably distributed among the poor people—indeed half of them were below the Poverty Line!

That is why she had popularized the slogan in one of her elections, "Garibi Hatao". Remove Poverty! Thus she had, with the assistance of her second son, formulated 20 points of economic rehabilitation of the backward communities—students, farmers, peasants, taxi-drivers, scooter-owner-workers, small craftsmen, pan-shops owners. This (on the advice of her Sanjay!) she had tied down with the apron-strings of the Emergency. During the year of the Emergency some good had been done no doubt, but the law-and-order excesses too had been committed and innocent persons—including sensitive women like Mrs. Primilla Lewis and Mrs. Snehlata Reddy, the well-known film actress of Karnataka—were arrested and apprehended, suffered all kinds of humiliations and indignities. The excellent plan of Family Planning, which is still one of the most beneficent and hygienically important social measure, was made. But forced sterilizations were misunderstood and misrepresented by the opponents of the

Government.

Addressing the International Conference of Women Scientists and Engineers in Bombay in September 1981, she said, first quoting the late Martin Luther king, Jr.: *"Our scientific power has outrun our spiritual powers. We have guided missiles and misguided men"*.

But she struck an optimistic note and said:

It is the search for truth, and the desire to apply knowledge for the benefit of the society in which they live that drives scientists on. Science and technology has given us a level of comfort and prosperity uudreamt of in earlier years even by the most affluent. We, in the developing countries, look to science not for luxuries but to solve such age-old problems as privation, and to bring about both greater social and economic justice and equality opportunity.

We need science for our immediate imperative of development—to improve efficiency, to produce more, to save time and labour, to reduce drudgery at all levels. And it is not just the big spectacular advances for which science is important, but the small improvements and adaptations, visible, and of immense immediate help, in every-day life, especially to the weaker sections of society. We want science in the humblest tribal hut; in our fields as well as in sophisticated industries and nuclear power plants . . . . .

"Science has not let us down. But sometimes it fills us with dismay to see how often science and technology have been used, unscientifically, for profit, or for some real or imagined success, that ignores the long-term chain reaction.

It was with these objectives that Indira Gandhi promoted such scientific projects as the Pokhran nuclear blast which opened the doors of Atomic Science being used for peaceful purposes; the release of gigantic *sputniks* crafted in India and released through courtesy of U.S.A. and U.S.S.R. (keeping parity of powers); the manufacture of Atomic Reactors for the generation of electrical energy and the like.

The training of two Indian astronauts—Rakesh Sharma and

Malhotra—and the close association of one of them with the advent of Soviet space science was the acme of perfection for the Indian young men!

The photographs received from this project were commissioned by Indian scientists and supplied to them by Soviet project officials.

It was the illustration of international cooperation by two equals in the community of nations.

The talk that Mrs. Indira Gandhi had with the Indian cosmonaut, Sharma, was the most shining moment of Indian capacity to probe the skies.

11

✾

Citizen of the World!

"The art of government has grown from its seeds in the
tiny city-states of Greece to become the political mode
of half the world. So let us dream of a world in which
all States, great and small, work together for the peaceful flowering of the republic of man."

ADLAI STEVENSON

SO FAR we have traced the personality of Indira Gandhi mostly
as an Indian leader. But that is not all.

She inherited her *cosmopolitan* world view (though not in the
sense in which the Soviets use the word as a kind of swear-word!)
from her father either by following his example, or by reading
his letters which are now printed together as *Glimpses of World
History.*

But a cosmopolitan, as I mean it and as based on Jawaharlal
Nehru's definition of Cosmopolitan, is a man of the *whole* world
—with the compassion and liberal-mindedness of the Hindus,
the courtesy and politeness of the French, the practical and technological mind of the German, the hospitality of the Arabs, the
frankness and open-ness of the Americans, and the patriotism and
friendly interest in all peoples and countries, and their cultural
and aesthetical level of the ordinary Russian—who, be he a Com-
missar or a humble Plumber, reads Tolstoy and Pushkin, and
loves to attend the Bolshoi Theatre.

A 'sophisticated' citizen to respect and love *all* the people of
all the countries, his cultural outlook must not be restricted to

any one culture and aesthetic but must embrace the whole world. This man—or woman feels at home in any country or city of the world, has no prejudices and partialities and has respect for other peoples of the world and their cultures.

"Do in Rome as the Romans do" is an old aphorism which has parallels in all the tongues of the world. "God's estate," the *Upanishads* say, "is deemed to lead to freedom, the demon's estate is Bondage. Grieve not, you are born in God's Estate." And the Holy Quran tells the Muslims to "pursue truth from the Cradle upto the Grave", and also to seek knowledge even if you have to go to China to acquire it.

Speaking on "The Man And The World" at the United Nations Conference on Human Environment,* she uttered a quotable quote when she said that *"Life is one, and the World is One"*. This inter-dependence of the whole world was the constant theme of Jawaharlal Nehru's internationalism he emphasized again and again everywhere from the International Forums to his village speeches in Uttar Pradesh.

Speaking at the same Conference she remembered "Edward Thompson, a British writer and a good friend of India, once telling Mahatma Gandhi that its wild life was fast disappearing. Remarked the Mahatma: 'It is decreasing in the jungles but it is increasing in the towns!'"

Later she says in the same speech:

We are supposed to belong to the same family, sharing common traits and impelled by the same basic desires; yet we inhabit a divided world.

How can it be otherwise? There is still no recognition of the equality of man, or respect for him as an individual. In matters of colour and race, religion and custom, society is governed by prejudice. Tensions arise because of man's aggressiveness and his notions of superiority. The power of the big stick prevails and it is used not in favour of fair play or beauty, but to chase imaginary wind-mills—to assume the right to interfere in the affairs of others, and to arrogate authority for actions that

*held in Stockholm on 14th June, 1973

[88]

would not normally be allowed. Many of the advanced countries of today have reached their present affluence through domination of other races and countries, and exploitation of their own masses and their own natural resources. Their sheer ruthlessness, undisturbed by feelings of compassion or by abstract theories of freedom, equality or justice, gave them a head start.

She quotes from her rational experience:

For the last quarter of a century, we have been engaged in an enterprise unparalleled in human history—the provision of basic needs for one-sixth of mankind within the span of one or two generations. When we launched into that endeavour, our early planners had more than the usual gaps to fill. There was not enough data and there were no helpful books. No guidance could be sought from the experience of other countries because their conditions—political, economic, social and technological —were altogether different. Planning of the kind which we were innovating, had never been used in the context of a mixed economy. But we could not wait. The need to improve conditions for our people was pressing. Planning and action, the amassing of data for improved planning and the action to implement it, was a continuous and overlapping process....

.... We should have a more comprehensive approach, centred on man, not as a statistic but as an individual, with many sides to his personality. These problems cannot be treated in isolation but must be regarded as an integral part of the unfolding of the very process of development....

She raises the eternal question of END and MEANS, and advances the view-point of an Oriental:

.... It is an over-simplification to blame all the world's problems on increasing population. Countries with but a small fraction of the world population consume the bulk of the world's production of minerals, fossil fuels and so on. Thus we see that when it comes to the depletion of natural resources and environmental pollution, the increase of one inhabitant in an affluent country, at his level of living, is equivalent to an increase of many Asians, Africans, or Latin Americans at their levels of living.

The inherent conflict is not between conservation and development, but between environment and reckless exploitation in the name of efficiency. Historians tell us that the modern age began with the will to freedom of the individual. And the individual came to believe that he had rights with no corresponding obligations. The man who got ahead was the one who commanded admiration. No questions were asked as to the methods employed, or the price which others had had to pay . . .

Ecology—the science of healthy environment in cities and towns—was ever near the heart of Indira Gandhi which was full of pride for the Indian scientists working in different fields including Space Research:

. . . . the ecological crisis should not add to the burdens of the weaker nations by introducing new considerations in the political and trade policies of rich nations. It would be ironic if the fight against pollution were to be converted into another business, out of which a few companies, corporations, or nations, would make profits at the cost of the many. Here is a branch of experimentation and discovery in which scientists of all nations should take an interest. They should ensure that their findings are available to all nations, unrestricted by patents. I am glad that the Conference has given thought to this aspect of the problem. . . .

The population explosion, poverty, ignorance and disease, the pollution of our surroundings, the stock-piling of nuclear weapons and biological and chemical agents of destruction, are all parts of a vicious circle. Each is important and urgent but dealing with them one by one would be wasted effort.

She quotes from the Vedas to effectively drive home the point:

[90]

.... He (Man) must again learn to invoke the energy of growing things and to recognise, as did the ancients in India centuries ago, that one can take from the earth and the atmosphere only so much as one puts back into them. In their 'Hymn to Earth', the sages of the *Atharva Veda* chanted:

What of thee I dig out, let that quickly grow over,
Let me not hit the vitals, or the heart.

She welcomed the New Representatives of Non-Aligned Movement in these words:

Many more nations have joined our family. What is the spirit that moves us? The spirit of national freedom. What is the common objective for which we work? Peace—which can only be achieved and preserved on the basis of political and economic equality among nations, the elimination of military domination and a determination to bring about disarmament.

She recalled the Founding Fathers of the Movement including her father:

This ennobling goal was bequeathed to us by the liberators and founding fathers of our various nations. They were, indeed, emancipators. The list of their names be long, and each is illustrious. But, to me, some stand out as examples worthy of special mention—Jawaharlal Nehru, Ahmed Soekarno, Gamal Abdel Nasser, Kwame Nkrumah and Josip Broz Tito. These are the few whose far-sighted vision nursed the concept, and nurtured the unity, of the non-aligned.

The Conference of the Heads of State of Non-Aligned Movement was one of those meets which provoked contrary reactions. The Oppositionists proclaimed the "useless" expenditure of Indian money on foreign guests. It is, however, plain fact that India owed it to the Movement to host one of the Conferences, whatever be the cost of it. It was not grander than the anniversary of the Iranian Kings to which many had been invited by the King

[91]

of Iran. But we owed it to the fact of Mrs. Indira Gandhi being Chairperson for the current session.
Several international Representatives arrived in Delhi.

We want to be friends with all. India's policy is to consoli-date friendship where it exists, where there is indifference, to create understanding and interest; and where there is hostility, to make every effort to minimise it. It is also our endeavour to find common areas, however small, between us and other nations, and to enlarge them.

Like a tutor of History, she told her audience:

Little did we imagine that the Cold War could so soon reas-sert itself. The thaw was short lived. Military alliances are now being refurbished. The danger of armed conflict increases. Clear enough reason for us to remain alert, to speak and work for peace....
.... The non-aligned movement originally developed in the context of a bipolar world. In the course of time other centres of power came up and used their military and economic capa-cities to bend the policies of newly-free, or small, countries to fit in with their own strategies. Today, even this multi-polarity is less in evidence.

She spoke with the authority of both Gandhi and Nehru when she issued this warning to those who were present:

Non-alignment is neither neutrality nor indifference. It in-volves the active and free exercise of judgement on certain principles. Peace is not passive. As a remarkable woman of my country, the poet Sarojini Naidu, said, 'True peace is not the peace of negation, not the peace of surrender, not the peace of the coward, not the peace of the dying, not the peace of the dead, but the peace of militant, dynamic, creative, of the human spirit which exalts.' Today let us concern ourselves with the future mobilising all our resources, material and moral, in our cooperative quest for such a peace.

Earlier there had been a grand gathering of Asian Youth in Delhi. It was Olympics on a slightly reduced scale. The appearance of thousands of sportsmen and sportswomen in the capital of India was a new phenomenon in Delhi. It was the first time that so many Asian youth got together. Their elders had got many opportunities to get together. Over a hundred nations had their representatives in India. Most of them had their experiences of the anti-imperialist political movement.

They met and talked—through English, unfortunately. But it was convenient as a weapon through which they conversed and felt at home in India. The ASIAD was more than a sports gathering. It was a God-given opportunity. It cost a lot—in inflation-ridden India!

The Prime Minister got her elder son nominated on one of the supervising Committees in which he worked with diligence and was never heard of having thrown his weight about. But he was now more and more identifying himself with India, and his mother Indira, and becoming a cheerful source of strength and inspiration.

By the time Asiad ended, the whole of the city of New Delhi was renewed and renovated, with numerous buildings which would make it possible to invite international meets and grand gatherings. The by-passes, the fly-overs, the new bridges and roads and the illuminated stadia are already enabling India to host international matches. Gandhian Economics and Austerity was no longer necessary or expedient. We were now a major power, and had to invite the meet of the Commonwealth Heads of State and the Conference of Non-Aligned Nations, for which the super-structure was now ready and tried during the ASIAD.

*   *   *

I would like to participate in a flight on a spaceship with a crew of young cosmonauts from different countries, including Russians, Indians and Americans. That would be a peaceful research spaceship.

The prophetic vision was of Yuri Gagarin, the *first* man in space, who, unfortunately, died soon after making a visit to India when he repeated his 'dream' again.

But his 'dream' lived on after him, when Indian space scientists crafted the spaceship, *Arya Bhatta* named after an ancient mathematician and scientist, who made his research and experiments which led to the possibility to send Man into space—crafted and built up by Indian scientists and engineers. And fired into space by Soviet boosters in Kozakistan.

Soon after was launched another satellite named after another Indian scientist, Bhaskar. Mrs. Indira Gandhi welcomed experiments of Bhaskara which were useful in practical fields of Forestry, Hydrology, snow-cover, Zoology, Land use and Ocean Surface. It is no use calculating the costs of these experiments and to say that so many schools and hospitals could be built with that money. Schools and hospitals are more important than Sputniks going into space, no doubt. But, under Rajiv Gandhi's Prime Ministership, we want money for both—the schools, the hospitals and latrines in villages and *also* for Space Research. The first Indian youth has been up in Space and has performed very well there, and now more and more young airmen in our Defence forces are rearing to go where only one Indian had gone before.

In this age of Science and Space we must include Space Research as an essential—as essential as modern defence forces.

What price Aryabhatta and Bhaskara if human sacrifice is still practised in India, if witchcraft is still practised, if irrational practices are still rampant in our land, and if sooth-sayers and quacks and witch-doctors are still plying their trade under the shadow of the man-made 'new star'.

12

Assassination !

"Common be your prayer,
"Common be your purpose,
"Common be your deliberations,
"Common be your desires,
"Common be your END."

—Old Sanskrit prayer

LATE IN the evening of 30th October, 1984, Mrs. Indira Gandhi returned from her 2-day trip to Orissa by an I.A.F. plane.

Accompanying her on this trip was the British writer-actor-director Peter Ustinov. In his T.V. serial called "Peter Ustinov's Personalities" was included a T.V. documentary on Mrs. Gandhi, for which the last interview, an elaborate affair, was to be recorded the next morning.

Mrs. Gandhi was particularly keen on giving the maximum cooperation for this film. That's why she had cancelled all her morning's engagements. She would not go to office that day, and she had agreed to walk across the road to 1, Akbar Road—the adjunct to the P.M.'s House in which her office was situated.

But Ustinov had come half an hour earlier and had set up his cameras on the lawns where a chair and table were placed for the convenience of the P.M.

It was nearing the time of appointment and Ustinov was not unnaturally in a sweat of anticipation. This session was the last of all his filming in Delhi—he had the P.M. doing every thing that habitually she was wont to do daily. He had had exclusive footage on her, which no other camera team had been able to get. He was anxious to fly on the morrow straight to London, where he would edit the footage for the final series. But everything was dependant on this crucial interview which would give the whole thing a touch of human informality for which he was famous.

Ustinov had been told that she was meticulous to the last detail and, in punctuality when she said it 9-15 meant 9-14 and 59 seconds.

But, unknown to Ustinov just across the road from her bedroom, as she emerged, she met two friends waiting for her. How's my make-up?" she queried displaying her *Gerva* sari and lightly rouged cheeks. "Is it all right for a T.V. camera?" she asked again and both the ladies agreed. But at that moment when she should have crossed the road to 1, Akbar Road, she instead rang the bell for her personal servant.

The servant came up running. "Yes, Madam," he inquired and waited for her instructions.

Mrs. Gandhi ordered tea with instructions that each lady's taste in sugar would be to her friend's satisfaction. The third cup was for her make-up artiste. Then she said, "Bye-Bye" to her friends and emerged from the side-door into the open courtyard.

She casually noted two of her Security guards there—She knew both of them well enough by names: Sub-Inspector Beant Singh and Jawan Satwant Singh who was a recent arrival.

At that moment she did not realise that they were not expected to be in the inner perimetre. In the light of the Extremist Sikhs' threats received by post and on phone, she herself had passed an order when questioned whether these two should be transferred to their original posts. She definitely remembered to have scribbled on their papers at the suggestion of the Head of the Security:

"Am I the Secular Head of a Secular Government or NOT?" That's all. Then she scribbled her initials—I.G. Thus they had remained—so what was amis in the little formality of coming in to the wrong perimetre. Perhaps the men who should have been there had gone somewhere else and these had taken their positions. They both bowed to her to *namaskar* her (the Sub-Inspec-

tor *salamed* politely) and she nodded to acknowledge their greet-
ings. Beant Singh was in her way, but he was following her movements. Suddenly she noticed the revolver in the Sub-Inspector's
hand as he finished *namaskaring* her.

"What *are* you doing with it?" she wanted to shout. "Do you
want to kill me?" but the question remained unspoken on her
lips!

The last thought that struck Mrs. Gandhi's mind was that this
action was parallel to that at Mahatma Gandhi's assassination.
That was how Godse had joined his hands with a revolver hidden
in them. Mrs. Gandhi heard the report of the revolver first. Then
she received the hit on her breast and slumped on the lawn.

The man who held an umbrella overhead was Narain Singh
who had taken up this task which had come down from the
Moghal etiquettes. Three other men were present on the lawn,
five to ten feet away from her. These included her personal
secretary, the all-powerful R.K. Dhawan, Rameshwar Das and
Nathu Ram. None of them was armed. Not even with a symbol
of authority.

But, surely, one would expect from these 'loyal' retainers some
action or reaction.

Her way was blocked by Satwant. The first murderous assault
had been made by Beant Singh. Before losing her consciousness
completely she heard a fusillade from Satwant Singh's sten-gun.
So it was he who had pushed the trigger and riddled with bullets,
showing no trace of mercy or compunction!

Sixteen bullets entered her body before the assassins called it
a day. They, the senior of the two, remarked "We have done
what we had to do, now you do what you want to do." Saying
this they entered their room.

What were the reactions of the three important men—Rameshwar Das, R.K. Dhawan and Nathu Ram? Did one of them at
least pounce on the assassins to disarm them or at least deflect
one of the bullets from its fatal and deadly course?

Meanwhile, the Prime Minister's elder daughter-in-law, Sonia,
rushed out of her room, gathered the prostrate, but still living
body lying unconscious on the lawn in a pool of her own red
blood, and carried it to the white Ambassador and rushed it to the

All India Institute of Medical Sciences.

The arrest of one Calcutta businessman, on the border of Nepal, with incriminating documents in his baggage, has added another dimension to the assassination conspiracy.

This arrest, however, has not yet yielded any results. But hope has not been given up and it may yet yield some clue to the conspiracy.

But there were other arrangements and these had been made for just such an emergency. There was a medical van kept standing at the house, but no one had thought of it. Also untried at that time was the radio transmitter directly connected to the main gate of the All India Institute of Medical Sciences! That is the cause of the delay of 10 precious minutes as the gateman failed to recognise the V.I.P. in the car.

Meanwhile, the British television team hearing the shots thought them to be the remnants of Diwali cracker outbursts. They kept waiting for the Prime Minister who was to die in the next two hours and would no longer give any appointments to visiting V.I.P. television teams! But along the grapevine, news spread that by a magical coincidence, the T.V. team had filmed the assassination on T.V. tape. But of course, that was not true!

The doctors, assembled for the supreme emergency, agreed that Mrs. Gandhi's life, though not her brain, could be saved. Still, various life-saving devices were used. Nothing worked. At half past twelve the senior surgeon shook his head in a gesture of finality. Thereafter, it was the futile function of post-mortem and embalming the body for the three days vigil. The bullet holes were stitched—there were twenty of them made both by revolver and sten-gun.

The senior assassin was killed by the Commandos in a scuffle —or something! It is not very clear or cogent. But there is no doubt that he was the king-pin of the conspiracy, and his absence has created a dubious question mark about the motives of the conspiracy. That, however, will never be known.

Whatever Satwant Singh will say and may say, will be limited and incomplete. He is but a boy. He will not be able to reveal all the angles of the conspiracy—that went to the cremation with Beant. The rest is with the others who controlled the conspiracy

—like the assassin of Liaquat Ali, Prime Minister of Pakistan, like the assassin of John Kennedy and Robert Kennedy! You hire two persons to kill and ensure that their secret will not be revealed! So it seems in this case!

At the time Mrs. Sonia Rajiv Gandhi was carrying the body of Indira Gandhi (her mother-in law) to the All India Institute of Medical Sciences, her husband was making a speech in far off Calcutta and wondering whether the Bengali peasants were getting the hang of it. Later, a Police Sub-inspector informed him that Mrs. Gandhi had been injured in a shoot-out. But he himself did not know the details. When flying to Delhi the pilot informed Rajiv Gandhi that the news of death was now confirmed.

The stoic calm of Rajiv Gandhi did not bare the absence of emotion. It was the outcome of the feeling that now the responsibility of guiding and leading the country was *his*. He could not afford to shed a son's tears.

That night, as he addressed the nation, he remarked that he had lost his mother along with all the people of India who had also lost their mother. So, he combined his grief with that of the people! He mourned his mother all the more because he did what she would have liked him to do—to do his duty. Thereby he fulfilled the aspirations of his people!

The mystery of his mother's assassination will remain a mystery for a long time. But the son is devoting himself to the affairs of the nation rather than be morbidly preoccupied with the mystery of his mother's assassination.

13

Verdict

"It is perhaps as difficult to write a good life as to live one."

—LYTTON STRACHEY

INDIRA NEHRU GANDHI!

Was she who was declared dead on 31st October 1984 at about 4 o'clock by the doctors at All India Institute of Medical Sciences "the Iron Lady of India"?

Was she the "Imperious Queen of Hindustan" as the London tabloids called her?

Was she the universal *Amma*, as the common people of South India called her?

Was she the reincarnate *Durga*, *Kali* or *Saraswati*, as some people called her?

Or was she "That Woman", as she was called by Yahya Khan, the Dictator of Pakistan?

Or was she the malevolent Dictator, a female version of Hitler and Mussolini, Peron and Zulfiqar Ali Bhutto, a sadist who imprisoned people and got them tortured and killed in her jails during the Emergency years?

Was she anti-Sikh as Hitler was anti-Jew, as some extremist Sikhs believe? Was she a Machiavellian politician, a cold-blooded tyrant?

Or did she have, like Roosevelt, five qualifications for statesmanship (a) courage; (b) patience, and an infinitely subtle sense of timing; (c) the capacity to see the very great in the very small and to relate the infinitesimal particular to the all-embracing general (though two of the great controversial issues eluded her —the Assam and the Punjab); (d) idealism, and (like her father) a sense of fixed objectivity; (e) ability to give objectivity. Also like Roosevelt she had plenty of bad characteristics—dilatoriness, two-sidedness (some critics would say plain dishonesty), pettiness in some personal relationships (as she was in throwing out Sanjay's wife, Maneka, along with her baggage) . . . . love of improvisation. . . . . . amateurism, and, what has been called 'cheerful vindictiveness' (again her relationship with her *bahu* Maneka comes to mind). Roosevelt (as well as *she*) was admired and loved all over the world . . . his (or her) appeal was universal.*

Did she take an unholy and psychotic pleasure in pursuing those she felt to be dangerous to her?

Was she religious to the extent of visiting every sacred temple and mosque or *tirth sthan* in India?

Was she a rationalist who did not believe in the rituals of Hinduism, like wearing a rudraksha *mala* and prostrating before the entrance of temples and gurudwaras and going to *rishis* and *swamis* and god-men?

Or was she a rationalist who once said to me that "Religion is a crutch for the infirm and the diseased!" Or was she misquoted?

Was she a typical Indian mother who loved her two sons more than any thing else in the world?

Was she corrupt in the sense of amassing untold wealth which she had deposited in *numbered accounts* in a Swiss Bank?

Was she a profligate who had umpteen lovers including sons of Maharajas, some Swamis and so-called Brahmacharis who had access to her bed-room at odd hours of the day or night?

Or was she cold and under-sexed who did not come up to the expectations of her own husband, who had to seek sexual relations with a number of married and single girls?

In short, was she a sinner or a saint? Did she serve her people with undisputed sincerety? Or was she all the time seeking Power for herself and her family?

Roosevelt in Retrospect by John Gunther, Hamish Hamilton. Words in bracket are added by K.A.A.

Was she a rationalist and socialist, something expected from a person to whom hundreds of letters were written by Jawaharlal Nehru which turned thousands of boys and girls into socialists and rationalists? Or is it true that she was not interested in those letters and carelessly threw them about? Is that why her 'socialism' and 'Secularism' was skin-deep?

Was he sufficiently (though without regularity and with odd gaps) educated, or was it that, like her sons, she may be regarded just a Matriculate, who had to get her speeches written by others?

Was she an Angel or a Devil? An original Angel who fell into the Power-game and went to the devil? Or was she originally a Devil who, through the influence of her father, became the Angelic Prime Minister of India and acquired all the graces of an Angel? Or are both the suppositions false?

While assessing the qualities of a historic personality like Mrs. Indira Gandhi, I am reminded of the late George Bernard Shaw who thought that the most intelligent man was his tailor who insisted on taking fresh measurements every time Shaw ordered a new suit to be stitched.

The personality of every man (and woman) is constantly evolving and changing, both spiritually and physically. So he must take fresh measurements every time. Perhaps, in a year or two, his height has risen by an inch or has gone down by half an inch. Perhaps he has grown stouter or slimmer. You can't say for certain that his clothes stitched several years earlier still give a perfect fit. That can be measured only by a tailor's tape.

So, psychologically and physically, Indu the daughter of the Indian Revolution, may have grown taller during one or another phase of her life. It is doubtful if she grew taller than 5 ft. 2 inches—that is physically speaking, when she was a slim, bashful girl in Anand Bhavan she was thin like a reed, and looked comic, dressed in boyish khadi *kurta pyjama* with a Gandhi cap on. Then she wanted to be martyred like Joan of Arc, but compromised with starting the *Vanar Sena*—the Monkey Brigade, to take on some of the minor courier functions as an ancillary of the National Movement. They would pass on letters from one to another leader. When she went to Europe with her father and wore long heavy coats with a black matching hat, with snow-boots to go to Madrid and Barcellona, she had a different personality—she looked much taller than she actually was. Back in India, when she married, the facial make-up and adornments with high-heeled shoes gave her a taller personality.

When she spoke from the Congress platform, due to optical illusion of those sitting under the rostrum, she looked much taller than even her father.

When she became Prime Minister, she acquired a new personality—seemingly tall, well-groomed with her hairdo and with the silverish streak in her black (or dyed) hair. She sat on a high chair in her office and she dominated those who sat opposite her across her desk. I have interviewed her and could not guess her height, while sitting opposite her.

The same about her personality in different moods and circumstances. When declaring the Bangla Desh victory* it was the highest water-mark of her personality and her political career.

This is about her physical personality! What about her psychological and emotional personality which seems to be elongated or shortened, according to her mood and circumstances!

When she was only a Minister for Information and Broadcasting, I met her with some other film producers at a meeting with her. She did not look tall and formidable! One felt that she was our equal. But by the time I sought an interview with her, she had become the Prime Minister and her personality had changed. She spoke as politely as before but, the way she accented her speech it acquired a strong inflection, as if suddenly she had taken on a dose of Power! When I complained about my not getting a reply to my letter written to her more than a month earlier, she flared up at her Press Secretary. "Do you see how your predecessor had landed me in misunderstanding with people I respect. I am sorry, Mr. Abbas, it was mischief of (naming the Senior Journalist who was her former Press Secretary), you know, I told him to send you a telegram saying I was available

---

*This occasion was important because one of the junior but gallant M.P.'s said that while others only made history, our Prime Minister had made *geography*, as well—because a new nation—of Bangla Desh—had been formed!

anytime you happen to come to Delhi, and that you were to ring him up".

I had another meeting with her when another senior Editor wanted Krishen Chander and me to join him at an interview with the Prime Minister. He had collected about a dozen journalists of the press in English and Hindi and we were supposed to persuade her on the matter of the selective release of Pakistani intellectuals—poets, writers and others—from among the nearly a lakh of Pakistani prisoners of war. I think she seemed to be relenting in her attitude when he dropped a brick by saying "The American press would also be happy with it!" That did it. "What do I care for the American press?" After that she spoke a tirade against the American press and what they were up to. Her whole attitude changed and she was entirely a different person. She looked to be growing taller than before.

I paused for a while after the others left. I wanted to apologise for my being present along with the others. I looked at her. Now she was not looking so ferocious, neither fatter nor taller. "About you and your veiws about Amerlca, I know and can trust you. Sometimes one has to shout and even abuse such people. It was mostly stage-acting."

"Then you gave a very convincing performance." She smiled and I said, "Good-bye, Mrs. Gandhi," and caught up with the rest of the delegates on the stairs.

I mean to say that for her it might be stage-acting, but it depended upon the mood you were in, and also her own mood. But generally I never heard her even raise her voice. She was as was her father—polite in the extreme, answering even tactless questions tactfully.

I think, in retrospect, that she was originally a very shy and a recluse sort of a person. But when she became Prime Minister one of her aides told her what Kamaraj had said about her being a *goongi gudiya!* (Dumb Doll). Abruptly, she decided not to be a *goongi gudiya* any longer. She knew then that her reticence was being misunderstood and misrepresented.

She was outspoken (which does not mean that she was rude to her elders) but from now onwards, she had a firm opinion of everything—whether in Parliament or in the Congress meetings. The image, changed almost overnight.

She was coming from Calcutta after addressing an evening meeting when she heard that Pakistan had bombarded the Indian airports. Her chauffeur was afraid of driving in the black-out with dimmed lights on. She assured him that she would take all the risks for rushing home at once, because she had already radioed the War Cabinet to be held at her house, and they must be waiting for her.

In her work, as Prime Minister, she had to meet all kinds of people—from visiting Heads of State to simple peasants who came for her *darshan* in the morning *Darbar-e-Aam*—General Audience—with some complaints about their village *patwaris*. It was her tact and compassion that both the Heads of State and the poor peasants left fully satisfied. The same was the case whether the V.I.P. happened to be American or Soviet Russian, without telling a direct lie, and feigning to be their exceptional friend, she more than satisfied both of them. This was also inherited from her father.

She had one weakness, though. It was the Indian mother's weakness. She was partial to her second son, Sanjay, and accepted as gospel truth whatever he told her and followed his advice, whether it was to destroy the houses in Turkman Gate or to appoint Bansi Lal as Defence Minister!

She tried her best to make me a Sanjay-admirer.* She told me he was a teetotaler, did not smoke or drink even Coca-Cola. During this conversation, Sanjay passed through the room where we were sitting, without wishing me or his mother. That gave her an occasion to talk all good things about him.

"If you like I will call him here to have a talk with you." I declined the "honour" with thanks.

I had written two letters to him so that I could visit his factory, because I wanted to write about it. He didn't reply to them. So I had no cause to welcome a meeting with him.

I think she was somehow 'afraid' of Sanjay because everytime I visited her house I often met Rajiv but never Sanjay.

That was her one weakness. But that is the emotional response

*During the last phase of the Emergency.

of every Indian woman. I had thought that she would rise above
it. But, due to her excessive much affection towards her younger
son this did not happen.

I think in all other respects, she grew up from a *goongi
gudiya*.

She was a frail and lonely woman who had very few friends
except Pupul Jaykar. When she needed them most she had only
one friend. When she was trounced in the election, Pupul, mostly
silent, kept her company, while she was waiting for her Cabinet
colleagues, most of whom had lost the election.

She kept herself busy, doing her work 16 hours of the day, with
a few hours of sleep.

She was polite to her official guests, very lively with foreign
correspondents. About Indian correspondents (with a few exceptions) she had an in-built prejudice. But she was most considerate
to the common people—especially Harijans and tribals. She
wanted to be an Anthropologist to study their lives and their
ways.

As she grew older she acquired some poise and dignity. She
became known to Heads of State and Government, especially in
the Third World countries, whose cause she was always espausing.

As her confidence grew, so did her style of oratory. Speech-
writers may have been writing her speeches, too, but it was always
her thoughts that she was articulating!

She was going to her house opposite where she had given an
appointment to Peter Ustinov, the British actor-director at 9.15
a.m.

She was 3 minutes too late when the assassin got her.

That story has already been told. But there is a report I
heard which I am repeating here.

There was a suggestion to remove these two guards (one was
a Sub-Inspector) because of the threats from Sikh extremists
which were regularly being received.

She is reported to have written on the file:

"Am I or am I not the Head of a SECULAR state?"

That's all. After that she initialled the report.

It was her own death-warrant that she herself signed!

Epilogue

Young Man in a Hurry !

As the "LAST POST" sounded its melancholy, yet haunting music, and the flames of the funeral pyre leapt up higher to touch the sunset-coloured sky, there was one youngish-looking man on whom all eyes were riveted. He was the Chief Mourner, being the only surviving son of the woman who had been assassinated two days ago.

The world leaders, from all important countries of the world, from both the power blocs, were there to share his grief. Two days ago, as he headed for Delhi, from a remote village in Bengal, he was almost whisked away straight to the Rashtrapati Bhavan, the President's Palace, for the swearing-in ceremony and to take the oath of office and secrecy. For while he was flying over India, from East to North-west, the Congress Parliamentary Party had met and unanimously elected the forty-year-old young man to be their leader and Prime Minister.

So he was the new leader of India, among the world leaders, receiving their condolences. That is why his own eyes were dry of tears. He could not afford to give an expression of emotional weakness. He had to be brave like his mother and his maternal grandfather. He could not afford to let down their traditions of courage and fortitude. He had to carry the burden of the problems of this vast country, which were many and variegated. The people had their trust in him. And, whatever his personal grief might be, he could not demonstrate it publicly.

Now he was a soldier at the front-line, with his duty to the people of India. That was what was meant by his oath of office. He was a symbol and a seal of office. Now his destiny was linked

[107]

with each one of the seven million people. He could not let them down. He could not also let down the community of world leaders of whom he was the newest entrant.

He must go to different countries—U.S.S.R. and U.S.A., to begin with—to take the measure of their leaders and let them take his measure. That was international protocol.

And so less than a week after his 6-day visit to the Soviet Union, and less than a week before he would, with his entourage of advisers, take off for U.S.A., I was in Room No. 1 of SOUTH BLOC of Lutyen's Secretariat, to keep my appointment with the new Prime Minister. I was sitting in his Press Advisor, Sharada Prasad's room, from where he rang up the P.M.'s Secretary to inform him that "Mr. Abbas has arrived and is sitting with me, he can be called any moment," without revealing to me whether the P.M. was in his office or on his way.

Soon I was summoned for my "tryst with destiny"—this was the third generation of Nehru-Gandhis that I was interviewing—I knew the corridor that I had paced with confident, young steps to meet Jawaharlal Nehru, then with a little feebler steps, to meet his daughter, Indira Gandhi, and today, when, at the age of 71, and I have to be supported by a stout stick, I was on the way to meet the youngest of them all.

I was looking ahead. I hobbled on my way when I was politely pushed aside to make way for the Prime Minister, with his half a dozen Security men. But the Nehru manners never cared for Security. It is a sign of the times, that the grandson of Nehru might be 'secured' by six men and sten-gun carrying men in the corridor, but the smile and the *namaskar* with which he greeted me was purely Nehruvian. Then he was gone in his room while I was ushered in his Secretary's ante-room and sat down for no more than a minute.

The desk before him was swept clean of papers and files which were always cluttering up the space in his mother's time. He again got up and out of his place behind the desk, and then he went back after shaking hands with me. Taking my time to reach the chair opposite his, I began by reminding him that the first time I really met him was at Amitabh Bachchan's Birthday Party, when Amit was working in my *Saat Hindustani*. He assured me that he well remembered the occasion.

Now, after this personal aside, it was time to begin the interview. So I asked for his over-all impression of the Soviet Union.

Q: *What is your impression of the Soviet Union?*

PM: The impression is *positive* in the work they are doing, the progress that they are making. Their leadership also seems to be very much attuned to developing faster, getting in the latest technologies, latest methods and really looking ahead. I have been to the Soviet Union thrice and each time I have found the living standards to be getting higher and higher.

Q: *And now,* I added, *you are going to the United States? What do you expect there—the same cordiality and friendship or something different?*

PM: The same.

Q: *The same?* I repeated his word and put a question-mark at the end of it.

PM: Yes. Our position on certain issues is well-known and then, we are not going to change our position whether it is on the Soviet Union or the USA. But there is no reason for there not being cordiality and friendship. Like I said, one of the things which is bothering us is Pakistan's nuclear programme. And, it appears to us that the USA is looking the other way, while they are going ahead with the programme. In certain places, like the Symington Amendment, it requires that the US government get an undertaking that to the best of their knowledge the country to receive military supplies or any major aid, is not developing a nuclear weapon. Now that amendment has been waived for only one country and that is Pakistan. That means that the US government feels, or implies....

Q: "....*partiality?* I suggested.

PM: Yes. And it feels that Pakistan cannot give a guarantee that they are not undertaking such a programme.

Q: *Did you ever have a fore-warning of your leap to destiny?*

PM: No. Not at all.

Q: *Did it come as a surprise to you?*

PM: Well, I mean, as a surprise in the sense that one thing led to another, led to another.

Q: *What were usually your uppermost thoughts, as you flew the night airmail AVROS, when I happened to meet you at Delhi and Nagpur airports. Were you ever involved in an accident or were you always a safe pilot?*

PM: Well, I wasn't involved in any accident. So you can say, I was a safe pilot. But it is not necessary that safe pilots don't have accidents. I mean, accidents are also due to other faults— mechanical, weather, other things beyond immediate control.

Q: *On October 31, 1984 when you were in a village in West Bengal, did you have a premonition of the importance of the day which cost you your dear mother's life, and catapulted you to the highest office in the country?*

PM: We were in a village. And it was normal, we got up, we went to the public meeting and just after the meeting we were given this news.

Q: *Not about the death but about the shooting?* I hinted.

PM: Yes. About the shooting. Well, even this, it was all very garbled and we didn't know any details at all.

Q: *How do you find the job now that you have been in office for more than six months? You are originally supposed to have a prejudice or dislike of the politics. Is it true? How do you find it now that you have experienced both politics and power?*

PM: Well, it is a responsibility. The people have trusted me to carry out certain programmes and to see that the country goes in the right direction and it is a tremendous challenge. I think that we have certainly taken a number of major steps which have helped in this process. And I believe India is really destined to go to great heights and we are in a position where we can start moving towards that now.

Q: *Are we really setting or we are hoping—for the path of progress?* I asked.

PM: Not hoping. We are!

Q: *What do you think generally of the job of the Prime Minister?*

PM: It is tremendously challenging and I am still sort of getting to know how Government really functions. Because I have not been involved in the complexities of bureaucracy and administration. So you do discover things!

Q: *Are there any road-blocks in bureaucracy and....?,* I ventured to ask.

PM: Well, there are vested interests everywhere, not only in the bureaucracy and you really have to work towards ending these vested interests.

Q: *What kind of vested interests?*

PM: I mean, vested interests in everything, and really in a *status quo* and not letting things change, a lot of inertia.

Q: *The vested interests are interested in keeping the status quo.*

PM: In everything. I mean, if it is in office procedure or if it is in a particular manner in which a file is to proceed, any change is resisted.

Q: *What do you think generally of the overall job of the Prime Minister? What should it be?*

PM: I don't understand. What should it be means what?

Q: *Should it be as a leader of men?* I explained, *or should it be following the popular trends?*

PM: Trend? I didn't mention that part because I thought that it was obvious. You have to be a leader, you have to show the way, you have to have certain ideas about where the country is going, you have to give positive direction, you have to be decisive.

Q: *What is your opinion of Jawaharlal Nehru. Have you read his books? Which do you like best?*

[111]

PM: I think, *Discovery of India* I like best. I think he was one of the greatest statesmen that we have had in our time. Certainly, maybe for a very long period. And he will go down as one of the all-time greats in human history. The vision, the thoughts, the ideology that he has left us is very very strong and powerful and not only for India but for the whole world.

Q: *What are your recollections of your mother*
(a) *as a mother and*
(b) *as Prime Minister?*

PM: As a mother, she was a mother in every sense, in every way, in her manner, in everything, affectionate, loving, very fond of the whole family, children and the grand-children.

As Prime Minister, I think she was courageous, strong, with very definite views on where India is going and nothing could swerve her from that path, no matter what challenges were thrown at her. Very clear about India's independence. India's .... really she believed in India.

Q: *Do you think,* I ventured to ask, *she had any authoritarian tendencies?*

PM: No, I don't think so at all!

Q: *What are your recollections of your father?*

PM: Loving us a lot, he had many hobbies and we used to be involved with him in those hobbies.

Q: *How old were you when he died?*

PM: I was 16.

Q: *...many hobbies and...?* I reminded him.

PM: ...a lot of interests, involved in a lot of things. He developed a similar sort of thinking, similar feeling. I think in both of us.

Q: *Did he take interest in your academic career or....*

PM: Yes. We were in boarding school at that time. From 1954 onwards I was in Boarding School.

Q: *And when your grandfather died you were in....?*

PM: When my grandfather died I was in the University.

Q: *Cambridge?*

PM: Yes.

Q: *What is your ambition as Prime Minister?* I asked a crucial question, *What is your image of India as its leader?*

PM: On the economic side, trying to remove as much of the poverty as we can and making India strong industrial nation. We have to compete with the rest of the countries in every major field.

On social side, to end the casteism, regionalism, linguisticism . . . all the 'isms' that we are encountering, to build up, to establish our own political position. To end all the ancient divisions that have existed in our society—discriminations against various groups whether they are Scheduled Castes or Tribes or women or backward or minorities, whatever.

Q: *Brides—they are burning almost one per day. Even if things can happen in the Capital then what will happen in the villages, in the towns and so on?*

PM: In fact, it is not happening so much in the villages, it is happening more in the towns. But that does not reduce the gravity of the situation and it has to be tackled. We are looking at it what to do with it. We passed a law last year. We have to take some more steps. And we will be doing some more things very soon. But these are not the things that can be removed by Governmental action. This has to be taken out of society. It is only with education and with better opportunity that it will go, more emancipation of women, better opportunities for women.

Q: *But don't you think the Government also has the responsibility to discourage this kind of thing, because it seems that the Congress leaders—their daughters are married and 16,000 people attended the marriage. This happened in Maharashtra and I mean, 10,000 or 8,000 or 6,000 are generally; I mean whole sports grounds are taken up and there being arranged and so many people coming.*

PM: I don't think the murders are directly connected with

this. I mean, they are two separate aspects. So, let us not confuse them. I am not condoning one for the other. But you cannot connect the bride-burning and bride-killing with this sort of ostentation which must be ended and curbed as well but the much more serious aspect is the burning of the brides.

Q. *But the ostentatiousness leads to bride burning?*

PM: No, not necessarily. I don't think so. Because the bride burning is murder, really. It is a different thing. They are really complaining not about the bride, but what they want from that family.

Q: *I meant that the ostentation also is a part of that budget.*

PM: Certainly it is. But let us not link the ostentation with the murder. That is what I am saying.

Q: ... *that the murder comes later?*

PM: As the murder is more important it comes first.

Q: *But nothing is done by the Government during the last so many years about these bride-burnings. There was no condemnation from the Prime Minister who was a woman!*

PM: I wouldn't agree there was no condemnation. I beg to differ with you. Numerous times, she has condemned bride-burning and atrocities on women. I think you have not been reading the newspapers, and you have been living in a little world of your own! In her last Parliament Session, we passed a Bill against this. I don't think you are aware of this.

Q: *I am aware. Last question: What is your definition of socialism? Because Jawaharlal Nehru said once that people will have to be, if necessary, forced, force will be applied for bringing about socialism, certain personalities or certain people are against socialism and therefore they will have to be forced into?*

PM: Well, the popular vote decides what is going to happen. If the people decide they want to go a certain path then that is the path the country goes. I think, to put it into a very short thing, Socialism is where the Government works for the people.

Q: *All Governments are supposed to work for the people.*

PM: Not necessarily. I don't think the American Government works for the people. Example says that they are working for the people; every action of theirs will be for the people. They say the people must work for themselves, by definition that is capitalism. The Government will do a certain amount and the people must do the rest. We say that basically all our actions will be to work for the people, whether it is running public sector, whether it is subsidising things for the poor, whether it is anti-poverty programme.

Q: *How do you plan to end poverty?*

PM: This is a very big question. I don't think it can be answered in the time that we have got. But basically, by making every sector much more active and more productive. Our largest sector is agriculture. So, obviously that is where we must start. But agriculture on its own cannot function. It needs industry to support it. It needs industry for power, for energy, for implements, for fertiliser, for everything. So, the whole thing really moves together. We must modernise, make it competitive; not just because we want to compete with the rest of the world but because we want to make it cheaper and better for our own people. One of the things we don't realise is when exactty we should try to save. Actually all the losses are being taken by the people, not by the Government and who is the Government? If you lose the money, it is the people. It is you and I and who is losing the money. Any inefficiency is loss for people. This we must check.

Q: *Are you aware that more than 50,000 villages have no drinking water?*

PM: Yes, I don't know the number but there are lot of ....

Q: *And how do you hope to remove poverty unless you give people drinking water at least, not bread but drinking water?*

PM: Do you think drinking water is more important than bread? I don't think the people in the villages think that.

Q: *They can drink any kind of water?*

PM: They would rather have the water they have been drinking and have some really, than have just pure water and . . . . Is it all right for you and I to sit when we have got everything and say "Drinking water", but there are other things which are more vital than drinking water. Drinking water is crucial. It is crucial to health, it is crucial to a million other things. But there are other things which are just as vital. So, we cannot just pick one item.

We could have given drinking water to everyone, maybe we would not have had roads, maybe we would not have had another million other things. It is a question of planning everything together. You can pick anything. We can say why everybody is not wearing shoes? But you can pick any one thing, of course, we could have done it. But we have to do it in one package where the whole spectrum is covered.

Q: *So, drinking water is not so important?*

PM: Drinking water is very important. But other things are also important. I, for example, would not pack up the whole of our defence system to give drinking water to all the villages because it would be counter-productive. Would it not? Because there are certain priorities you have to give. For example, would you sacrifice the whole immunisation programmes for children instead of drinking water? So, these are all trade offs. I mean you have to make a balance, you have to make a balanced plan.

Q: *Thank you.*

I had deliberately provoked him, but I came away with an impression of a young man in a great hurry.